The Art of
ANNEMIEKE MEIN
Wildlife Artist in Textiles

The Art of

ANNEMIEKE MEIN

Wildlife Artist in Textiles

SEARCH PRESS

First published in paperback in Great Britain 2001
Search Press Limited
Wellwood, North Farm Road,
Tunbridge Wells, Kent TN2 3DR

First published as hardback in Australia 1992
by Penguin Books Australia Ltd.
First published as hardback in Great Britain 1994
by Search Press Ltd.

ISBN 0 85532 977 7

Suppliers

If you have difficulty in obtaining any of the materials
and equipment mentioned in this book, or if you would
like further information on other titles published by
Search Press, then please visit the Search Press website:
www.searchpress. com

Alternatively, you can write to the publishers at the
address above, for a current list of stockists, which
includes firms which operate a mail-order service.

*To my husband, Philip, for supporting my
artistic development with patience,
encouragement and love, while remaining my
best friend and adviser. And to our two
children, Joanne and Peter*

Illustrations on preliminary pages:
Endpapers: No. 13, *Dragonflies*, detail
Page i: No. 54, *Dance of the Mayflies*, detail
Page ii: No. 42, *Freedom*, detail
Page vi: sampler for No. 40, *Early Birds*

Front cover:
No. 24, *Pink Emperor Gum Moth II*, detail

Back cover:
No. 57, *Lewin Honeyeater Nestlings I*, detail

Page 158:
No. 57, *Lewin Honeyeater Nestlings I*, detail

Opposite:
No. 56, *Frog Down Under*, detail

Printed in Spain by Elkar S. Coop, 48180 Loiu (Bizkaia)

CONTENTS

Foreword: Charles McCubbin   viii

List of Works   xi

Profile: Phillip Mein   1

Author's Note   7

Textile Works   11

Acknowledgements   159

FOREWORD

Years ago my father made the comment, 'All great art is the combination of rare skill *plus* imagination', a comment I never forgot. Good craftsmanship is relatively common, but real imagination is scarce indeed. To know Annemieke is to be conscious of a rare imaginative gift that pervades everything she does. The first time I went to a dinner party at the Meins' and experienced her exquisite cooking, I also found that each guest had their place marked with a Blue Gum leaf on which names were sewn in flowing script.

I first heard of Annemieke's work through my daughter, who had been invited to the Meins' while she was working at the Sale hospital. She couldn't stop talking about Annemieke's work when she returned home. The Mein family duly came out for a barbecue lunch, while I was building my studio at Longford over Easter 1979. I expected to have much in common with another wildlife artist, but, within minutes of our first meeting, it was the discovery that we both had a lifelong interest in invertebrates that made the occasion so memorable.

Much of the wildlife art I see is repetitious: nearly all of it is confined to vertebrates and flowers, with lots of 'birds on twigs'. While not wishing to denigrate the many excellent artists working in this field, much of their art seems to say to the viewer, 'I am copied from a photograph or a museum specimen: I am dead!'. The world of invertebrates is largely ignored, even though invertebrates represent 90 per cent of all animals. Many people regard anything with more than four legs as something to be feared, or killed on sight.

Annemieke's contribution to wildlife art is therefore important. In portraying insects so much larger than life, she has opened a window on the world that surrounds us, a world that is beautiful, fascinating and mostly unseen. The love and understanding that shine through her work are based on long hours of observation and study. Countless insects have been reared in her studio, their life cycles observed and documented with beautiful drawings.

Sawflies is a typical example. Annemieke has described in the text only one aspect of all the observation and documentation that preceded her work. She has told me about some of the other things she learnt – how the larvae communicate with each other by tapping the stems and leaves with the tips of their abdomens as they disperse from their daytime clusters to feed on gum tips at night. Throughout the night they keep in touch by this means, finally changing the tempo when it is time to regroup into clusters as dawn approaches. She also noted that the larvae appear to need moist soil before they can burrow down to make their underground cocoons. From a biological point of view, this probably explains how climate can limit their breeding.

Annemieke's work is not confined to insects. The same meticulous observation and detailed drawing precedes all her work, whether it be birds, frogs, barnacles or anything else. In 1979 she had already taken work in textiles in a new and innovative direction. She had demonstrated that textiles could be used as an exciting sculptural medium. Those familiar with her work thought of her only as an artist, but because she was working in textiles, she always ran the risk of being lumped together with other craftworkers. I was delighted when she accepted the commission to make six bas-relief bronzes for the Wall of Fame in the new Sale pedestrian mall. This firmly established her reputation as an artist and sculptor. Since then she has gone from strength to strength as she explores and develops new techniques in her use of textiles and fabric paints.

Underpinning all her work is a rare standard of craftsmanship. Annemieke would qualify as an artist of note for the quality of her drawing alone. The dozens of exquisite drawings that are part of the groundwork for all her major pieces are gems in their own right. All her important works are preceded by carefully drawn cartoons, in which all the tonal values are rigorously assessed, including the shadows cast by relief sections.

For artists who work on flat surfaces, producing convincing perspective drawings of the abstract patterns on the bodies of animals or the wings of insects is difficult enough. It is much more difficult to judge the right amount of distortion or foreshortening needed to enhance a three-dimensional illusion, particularly when some of the surface is in partial relief and has some perspective in its own right that will vary with the viewing angle. I have watched Annemieke when she has been working on this problem and have seen how many times she has made individual elements, tried them in place, altered or remade them, until she was satisfied that they looked right. The finished work gives no hint of the effort required to achieve the effect. Similarly, the misplacement by a millimetre or one degree of even the smallest item in a large work can spoil the balance of the design. Annemieke spends hours getting it exactly right, using paper cutouts as models. She checks the placement of each part by viewing the work on the wall, on the floor, and in a mirror, until she is absolutely certain that the final effect is what she wanted to achieve.

I am sure that those who are not themselves artists seldom appreciate how difficult it is to produce a balanced and satisfying work of art. These days many artists pay little attention to the lasting quality or compatibility of the materials they use — their work will not survive long. Annemieke goes to quite extraordinary lengths to ensure that her work will last. All the materials and colours she uses are exposed to full sunlight for long periods to ensure that they are durable and will not fade. She consults a leading conservator of art to ensure that nothing has been overlooked.

Annemieke is the most thorough and meticulous craftsman I have met. It is her craftsmanship that is the foundation for her artistry. She is also the only woman to whom I can present a branch covered in hairy caterpillars and know that it will be well received.

Charles McCubbin

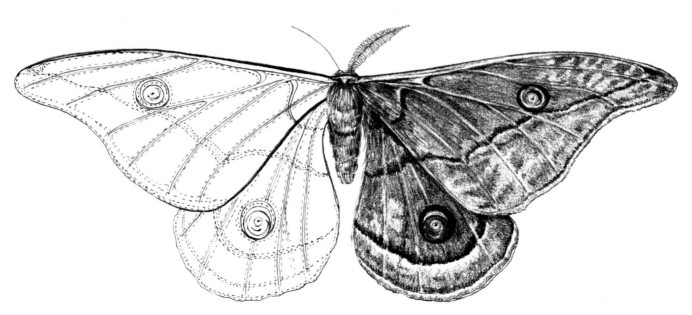

Emperor Gum Moth stitch plan.

—LIST OF WORKS—

1 White-faced Heron 12
2 Coastal Banksia 14
3 Eastern Water Dragon 17
4 The Morass – Sale 19
5 Bush Jacket 21
6 Maternity Dress 21
7 Dragonfly Cape 23
8 Lacewing Vest 24
9 Butterfly Ties 25
10 Fisherman's Tie 25
11 Grasshoppers 26
12 Frogs 30
13 Dragonflies 32
14 Cup Moths 34
15 Cup Moth Larva 36
16 Sawflies 38
17 Superb Blue Wrens 41
18 Christmas Beetles 43
19 The Potter Wasp I 45
20 The Potter Wasp II 46
21 The Old Lady Moth 49
22 Squabbling Gulls 51
23 Pink Emperor Gum Moth I 54
24 Pink Emperor Gum Moth II 56
25 Above the Channels 59
26 The Nest 63
27 Case Moth Cocoons 64
28 Emerald Moth on Banksia 66
29 Fallen Red Gum Log 69
30 Fallen Branches 70

31 Silvereyes 73
32 Ameinus McCubbinonymous, Lepidoptera 77
33 Mythical Moth 78
34 Mating Mythical Moths 81
35 Slate Pencil Sea Urchin 85
36 Barnacles 88
37 Mussels and Kelp 90
38 Wattle Seed-pods 92
39 Here She Comes! 94
40 Early Birds 98
41 Lepidoptera Quadripartite 100
42 Freedom 104
43 Freedom Samplers 106
44 Night Flight 112
45 Fantail Rhapsody 115
46 Fantail Night Watch 120
47 Southern Blue Gum Blossoms 122
48 Flight Dust 124
49 Butterfly Dust 126
50 Pittosporum Seed-pods 128
51 Pittosporum Blossoms 129
52 Fabric Fantasy 131
53 Grasshopper Flight 135
54 Dance of the Mayflies 136
55 Mayfly Life Cycle 140
56 Frog Down Under 143
57 Lewin Honeyeater Nestlings I 146
58 Book on Lewin Honeyeater Nestlings II 150
59 Lepidoptera Olympia Australis 152
60 Pheromone Frenzy 154

OPPOSITE Sketches and textile sculpture for No. 27, *Case Moth Cocoons*.

PROFILE

The artwork of Annemieke Mein is unique. She combines fabric, paint and sewing threads to produce works that are realistically accurate but that also breathe with life and action, and are emotionally breathtaking for the observer.

Annemieke's art is difficult to categorise. Textile work has traditionally been 'craft', but Annemieke has moved it into the world of 'art'. As one writer has noted:

The line between art and craft is being bent and breached these days, but there are only a few practitioners who can make it disappear completely.

The astonishing work of Annemieke transcends these and a few other categories besides. Embroidered and painted relief tapestries and fabric sculptures also erase the distinction between naturalistic and impressionistic portrayal.

Black and white photos cannot hope to do this work justice. In situ, one is first startled by her amazing mimicry of nature. A furry moth on brown bark, for instance, both invites and repels the tentative touch of those who are squeamish around insects. A strand of kelp hung with mussels is so real that one is tempted to throw it back into the water.

Having recovered from an intoxicated admiration of this virtuosity, you then begin to appreciate the artistic decisions which raise these works above sober actuality. They sing with her love of nature. They are magnifications [of] and heightened insights [into] nature . . . Annemieke Mein does not anthropomorphise her subjects or clothe them in whimsy. Her vision manifests itself in decisions to magnify a subject and subtly stylise it; in composition, in painterly renderings of the things which surround or lie beyond the focal point.

Textile paints are used in conjunction with complex machine and hand stitching, to create effects which are sometimes astonishingly like watercolours, sometimes like impressionistic oils. Black or sepia stitching is used like the most delicate pen work. In some works the distinction between painterly and sculptural rendering is also erased. (John Clare, *Sydney Morning Herald*, 31 May 1984)

Annemieke was the first textile artist to be accepted as a member of both the Wildlife Art Society of Australasia and the Australian Guild of Realist Artists. In 1988 she had similar works touring Australia in both art and craft exhibitions. The sculpture *Mussels and Kelp* travelled with the Bicentennial exhibition 'The Face of Australia', and the sculpture *Barnacles* was included in the Ararat Gallery's 4th Biennial Exhibition of Fibre and Textiles. She remains the only textile artist to be featured in *Australian Artist* (March 1987).

Annemieke's work has come into being with a special combination of uncommon abilities and circumstances. She has superb drawing skills, together with a highly developed sense of colour, and a feeling for composition and light and shade. These would have been sufficient for her to have become an accomplished artist in painting or sketching, but they have been combined with a love for, and a knowledge of, the properties of textiles, sewing skills, and an intense interest in the natural world around her. Her ability to observe, experiment and learn; her clever organisation of her limited time, housework and family life; her systematic storage of fabrics; and her freedom in the early years from having to produce work for a quick sale have all contributed to the quality of her work.

Annemieke was born in Haarlem, Holland, in 1944 when Germany still occupied Holland. She and her parents became Australian citizens in 1956. They migrated to Australia in 1951 when she was seven, leaving behind food shortages, rationing and the general chaos of war-torn Europe. In Holland she had spent much time with her mother's parents and felt very sad to leave them. She never saw them again.

A difficult transition period followed. There was a traumatic and protracted journey to Australia. After a short stay in the Bathurst migrant camp, the family moved to Bowral, NSW, then to Brighton in Melbourne, Victoria.

Annemieke was thrust into a State primary school unable to speak English. Her parents worked long hours to get established. An only child, Annemieke had many hours to herself but she put them to good use. She was fascinated by the plants, insects, birds and animals in Australia, so different from those in Holland. As a New Australian, she took nothing for granted. In those pre-television days, and with no brothers or sisters to share her time, beetles, birds, spiders

Annemieke at eight, with her first sewing machine.

and other inhabitants of the Australian landscape became her friends. She studied and sketched them.

Later, when her parents could afford a car, then a boat, the family went fishing and holidaying; again Annemieke amused herself by delving into the Australian landscape and collecting specimens, some of which she still has. She has always been an avid collector. She has collections of shells, stamps and hatpins, tins of buttons, lots of pressed wildflowers and leaves, butterflies, insects, feathers, nests and rocks.

Annemieke's mother is a skilled dressmaker, with a good sense of colour and a flair for interior design. Annemieke either learnt or inherited these skills too. Her father is an advanced dental technician. Annemieke spent time working in his dental laboratory and followed his example of high standards in the precise manufacture and finish of dentures, plates and metalwork. He also demonstrated artistic skills in manufacturing prostheses such as artificial eyes, noses and ears requiring careful texture and colour matching, and later in some bronze sculptures of his family.

Annemieke attended Brighton State School, Mitcham State School, and Nunawading High School. She continued to sketch and draw during this time and took art as a subject in her Matriculation year. Not surprisingly, she was a star pupil and her art teacher encouraged her to become a secondary art and craft teacher herself. She started

training at the Melbourne State College. However, she was unable to accept the abstract art that was in vogue at that time and she left after only three months.

Annemieke then pursued a nursing career, training at the Royal Melbourne Hospital, graduating in 1967. She subsequently trained in coronary care nursing and theatre nursing. Nursing enhanced her interest in biology and has helped her overcome any squeamishness she might have felt in her collection and dissection of specimens.

Annemieke and I met at the Royal Melbourne Hospital and were married in 1968. We moved to Sale in 1971 with our six-month-old daughter, Joanne. Our son, Peter, was born in 1972. For some years Annemieke was fully occupied with two small children and the demands heaped on her as the wife of a country general practitioner. But when she decided she wanted to return to nursing, she found that the policy at the local hospital was not to employ the wives of visiting medical staff. So she threw herself into a large number of crafts in a search for a meaningful and satisfying outlet for her creativity. She dabbled in painting and drawing. We still have many pieces from her year or so of doing pottery. Her macramé used to hang all over the house. She made gift cards, lace, and then lace pictures. She also made pictures out of bird feathers, and later out of bark. Knitting and crochet, spinning and weaving, clay modelling and papier-mâché, leatherwork, jewellery-making, paper-making, découpage, patchwork quilting, felting, dressmaking, etching, and restoration of old furniture were all experienced and mastered. Her flair for interior design was put into the house and into some friends' houses. Perhaps it was her experience with hand embroidery (ranging from traditional cross stitch to crewel embroidery), and fabric collage work, that led later to machine embroidery.

She was expert at this myriad of crafts and her work was widely sought after for craft exhibitions. It seemed, however, that these crafts did not satisfy her artistic creativity, unlike her textile pictures and sculptures.

Annemieke started to experiment with textile pictures in 1977. She would now regard those first works as very primitive. Some of them were copies of other designs, or simple drawings translated into textiles. It was during 1978 that she really started designing wildlife pictures herself, and then executing them in textiles.

She achieved national recognition in 1978, winning the inaugural Family Circle/Coats Patons Craft Award. From many thousands of entries in every conceivable type of craft throughout Australia, the judges selected Annemieke's *Coastal Banksia*. First prize was a trip to New York, but more important than winning this was the formal

Annemieke at work on *Fantail Rhapsody*.

recognition of her artistic achievement, spurring Annemieke on to produce more work.

At that time she established the work pattern that she still keeps. The housework is finished by the time the children go to school, then she goes into the studio upstairs for hours of concentrated artwork. Motherly duties take over again after school, but often she manages a few hours after the evening meal for tying off threads, or preparing for the next day's sewing.

Her first major exhibition was 'Invited Gippsland Craftsmen' at the Sale Regional Arts Centre in 1979. She exhibited about eighteen works, and the public response was incredible. Her work evoked a strong emotional response and many people were moved to tears. They returned with their husbands or wives, their children, their workmates and their friends. The question put by an artist friend, 'Why do you work in textiles, which take so long, when you can paint and draw so well?' was answered. Perhaps people's familiarity with textiles and sewing in clothing, curtains and bedding enabled them to relate to the works more easily than they could to paint. Perhaps Annemieke's larger-than-life portrayals of her subjects, or the three-dimensional studies, or the textural effects of the fabric were important. Whatever the reasons, her reputation was established.

She has had exhibitions at the Sale Regional Arts Centre every year since 1979. The Director there until last year, Mrs Gwen Webb, has been an important and encouraging influence on Annemieke. Mrs Webb is also intensely interested in Gippsland's natural environment, and in educating the community about its importance. Mrs Webb recognised the public appeal of Annemieke's work, and since then the Sale Regional Arts Centre has acquired a large number of her textiles. Some have been continuously on display since 1979. Mrs Webb also encouraged Annemieke to make audiovisual aids in the form of synchronised slide films of several works – *Superb Blue Wrens*, *Grasshoppers*, *Frogs* and *Small Works in Textile*. These are widely used – at the Sale Regional Arts Centre, at other exhibitions, and for education in schools and colleges. They show the way a textile picture or sculpture is created from start to finish. Annemieke does not believe in keeping any so-called 'trade secrets' from others, and encourages students to try her techniques. She regularly holds teaching workshops, and Schmeling Art Video Australia has made a commercial video on her work methods.

Annemieke met Charles McCubbin in 1979. He moved from Melbourne to the Sale area shortly afterwards. As a naturalist and as an artist he has been of immense help to her. He is a mine of information on Australian wildlife, especially insects, and willingly shares his knowledge, some of which is not yet recorded in books. In the early days of Annemieke's career, his encouragement and approval of her work gave her great incentive to continue. It was also the start of a close and enduring friendship.

Annemieke was given a Husqvarna Class 20 sewing machine for her eighteenth birthday by her parents. This was the machine that she used on her early pieces and it was particularly suited to the 'free-sewing' technique she developed. Husqvarna have been very supportive of Annemieke, and have supplied later-model sewing machines for her own use, and also sewing machines for the students in her workshops. In 1982, with Husqvarna, she exhibited and demonstrated at the Swedish Trade Fair at Centrepoint in Sydney, and was presented to King Carl XVI Gustaf of Sweden.

In 1980 Annemieke exhibited *Frogs* in 'Australian Crafts 1980', the Centenary Celebration Exhibition at the Meat Market Craft Centre in Melbourne, and it won the inaugural Hoechst Textile Award. As with Husqvarna, she has enjoyed a very happy relationship with Hoechst Australia Ltd. She uses their pigments in fabric paint, they have twice reported her work in their *Hoechst Report*, and they have helped with the costs involved in printing catalogues for her exhibitions at the National Gallery of Victoria in 1981, and the Woolloomooloo Gallery in 1984.

Perhaps the most important exhibition Annemieke has staged was at the National Gallery of Victoria for their Department of Education Services. Called 'Environmental Textiles', it was officially opened by Dr Eric Westbrook on 14 October 1981. Annemieke further developed the ideas that she had started using at her exhibitions in Sale. Not only were there finished works on display, but there was a large amount of supporting educational material as well – initial sketches, working designs and layouts, colour plans, threads and fabrics used, and notes on her techniques. There were synchronised slide films showing how the works were made, mounted specimens, and a catalogue for schoolchildren to improve their observation and knowledge of the flora and fauna portrayed.

The National Gallery exhibition ran for six weeks and was a resounding success. Enormous numbers of people saw it. The response was a magnified version of the response to her Sale exhibitions but from a more sophisticated audience. There was a flood of letters of congratulations from an admiring public. Since then, many of these admirers have travelled hundreds of kilometres, often in busloads, to view her exhibitions in Sale.

Another important exhibition was the 'Annemieke Mein Retrospect 1979–1984', which coincided with the Australian Pacific Embroidery Festival. It was held at the Woolloomooloo Gallery, Sydney, in 1984. The owners, Elinor and Fred Wrobel, invited Annemieke to show her work there in a non-commercial exhibition. Again, it was very successful.

The Annemieke Mein Retrospect 1979–1984 at the Woolloomooloo Gallery attracted 10,000 visitors from the country, interstate and overseas during three weeks . . . The reactions were awe, admiration, adulation and unrelenting questioning about her work, techniques, personality and philosophy. (Elinor Wrobel, *Textile Fibre Forum*, Vol. 3, No. 3, 1984)

Annemieke took a giant step sideways in 1984–85 when she was persuaded to design and produce six historical bas-relief bronzes for the Wall of Fame in the new pedestrian mall in Sale. They feature the portraits and lives of Alfred William Howitt (1830–1908), Mary Grant Bruce (1878–1958), Ada Crossley (1871–1929), Allan McLean (1840–1911), Angus McMillan (1810–65) and Nehemiah Guthridge (1808–78).

The Wall of Fame concept was initiated by Cr Peter Synan, Mayor of Sale. It was a brave commission for her to accept as she had never worked in bronze before. It also reflected the City of Sale's confidence that Annemieke would bring the same high artistic standard to the bronzes that she brought to her textiles. She studied the techniques required for bronze, and meticulously researched the lives of the people she was depicting. Mayor Peter Synan later wrote: 'These bronzes are an extraordinary achievement, constituting artwork of the highest order' (*Reflecting Gippsland*, Enterprise Press, 1985).

In 1987 the Sandhurst Trustees in Bendigo and the Bishop of Sandhurst commissioned Annemieke to produce a similar bas-relief bronze sculpture depicting the life of Dr Henry Backhaus (1812–82), the first priest to go to the Victorian goldfields (at Bendigo). The sculpture now hangs in the Backhaus Arcade in Bendigo.

In 1990 Annemieke exhibited her work with the Department of Entomology, CSIRO, Canberra, during Biota '90. The huge crowds who attended appreciated the juxtaposition of the scientific displays and Annemieke's artistry. She also exhibited at the Castlemaine Art Gallery during the Castlemaine State Festival. The gallery director, Mr Peter Perry, confirmed that this was the most popular exhibition ever held there. Mary Lou Jelbart wrote that 'Annemieke Mein's three-dimensional creations are works of extraordinary skill, born out of a passionate commitment to the environment that she observes with such a loving eye' (*The Age*, 21 November 1990).

The City of Sale honoured Annemieke with a civic reception in 1985 to celebrate her artistic services to the region. They also nominated her for an Australian honour and in 1988 she was awarded the Order of Australia Medal 'for services to the Arts, particularly in textile sculptures and bronze bas-relief sculptures' in the Queen's Birthday Honours. It was a fitting tribute to a remarkable woman.

Phillip Mein

27.5.'82.

eliminate stick or have it + form leaf
as a "separate".

frill —
- accentuate cocoons' frill/
attachment/opening
- sew separately and
conceal joins in pleats.

Sew rough puckery stitches that
pull in + naturally distort the
fabric. See specimen. Simulate
textured look of old cocoon
silk.

darts/pleating/gathering to obtain
wrinkly look at neck — both
vertically and horizontally.
Rough guide trial — assess
size of textile cocoon at its
widest point.
- allow for seams
- add width of vertical pleats
(Do a trial drafted pattern)

differ the shades in the cocoons
- underlay fabrics (wools,
threads, dacron etc)
ie. darker tones to natural
shadow areas.
- machine emb. with darker
and lighter threads as
above.

Horizontal gathering: measure
neck length, add 4" plus depth
of pleats.

Sticks blend into the
cocoons' silk — see
specimen.

sticks —
- accentuate attached sticks for
added visual impression.

- texture with varying tensions of
stitching and colour tones.

- machine in tubes ⟶ reverse
- stuff with dacron/wool/? stiffen.
? millinery wire

- unobtrusively thin end
with internal darts

- hand sew closed — vary shape of
end finish

- conceal darts with
sticks if necessary

- hand attach.

- lengthen ⟶ widen trail twigs proportionally
to cocoon design

AM

Working sketch for No. 27, *Case Moth Cocoons.*

6

AUTHOR'S NOTE

The encouragement of an awareness of our environment and an understanding of the importance of the preservation of our natural heritage are among the most important needs of our time. Gippsland, where I have lived for twenty years, still has a rich diversity of flora and fauna. It covers about one-sixth of Victoria, and its habitats range from snowy high plains and plateaus to forests, grasslands, inland lakes, rivers, wetlands and beaches. Man's use of the natural resources of this region – its oil, natural gas, coal, timber, water and the soil itself – together with the accompanying population growth, will inevitably have a profound effect on the survival of its wildlife. I have already seen disturbing changes in the environment and witnessed the effects of apathy, ignorance, financial greed and premeditated vandalism.

Through my textiles, whether sculptures, wall works or 'wearables', I hope to make people more aware of our native species while expressing my love and concern for our natural environment. My art has evolved through my lifelong interest in Australian flora and fauna. I still use any excuse to go out in the field and always feel rejuvenated when I do so. Each work requires extensive research, field studies, observation, specimen collecting, countless sketches and a disciplined timetable of working hours.

Insects are my primary interest. With the aid of fish tanks, boxes, jars and netted cages I have been able to successfully breed many of them and observe their complete life cycles. This has given me deeper insight into their particular characteristics and behaviour and assisted me in portraying them in original and credible ways.

I study species of birds, frogs and lizards in the wild, then sketch, photograph and research them further through library references. From time to time mounted specimens have been borrowed from museums and collectors, and live specimens have been lent by breeders. Many an unfortunate road victim has been delivered to me by a supportive local community member.

My textile works generally portray indigenous Australian species. Although many are realistic in style, they are not correct in every botanical or anatomical detail. Instead, they try to capture an event or experience, and the mood or emotion that the subjects have aroused in me. The works are also designed to have a strong visual impact through larger-than-life relief dimensions, textural variations and colour combinations. I especially enjoy depicting species that are not normally considered interesting, let alone beautiful, and visually enhancing their individual charms and attributes by giving a great deal of attention to their fine details. The sculpture *Cup Moth Larva* is an example. This is a grub to be wary of – its bristles give a nasty sting – yet I have chosen to feature the beauty of its multicoloured saddle.

Sketching has also been a lifelong interest. My initial sketches are quick and simple, and are intended only to capture an action, antic or behavioural pose. Full-scale work layouts and plans, however, can take weeks to prepare before I begin a textile.

Designing a textile on paper is very different from executing it in fabric, because I have to allow for the light and shade created by the relief work, and the textures of the various materials. It is also easy to clutter a work with too much detail in the sewing and knowing when to stop is a learned art. I prefer designs that look simple, yet their making may be extremely complex.

Often the colours used are not identical to the real species, as I prefer to alter colour tones to suit the mood and purpose of the design. In my early work I preferred the soft muted colours of our bush and landscape and generally used brighter pigments very sparingly. Splashes of colour were only introduced on focal points, such as the inside of a bird's beak or on the wing of an airborne insect. In later years I have enjoyed using a wider range of colours, particularly in my imaginative and interpretational works, such as the Mythical Moth series. I have also used paint more extensively as a colour-tone basis for embroidery, both on the backing canvas and on the fabric of the sculptures.

The materials used, such as silk, wool, fur, cotton and synthetics, are carefully chosen for

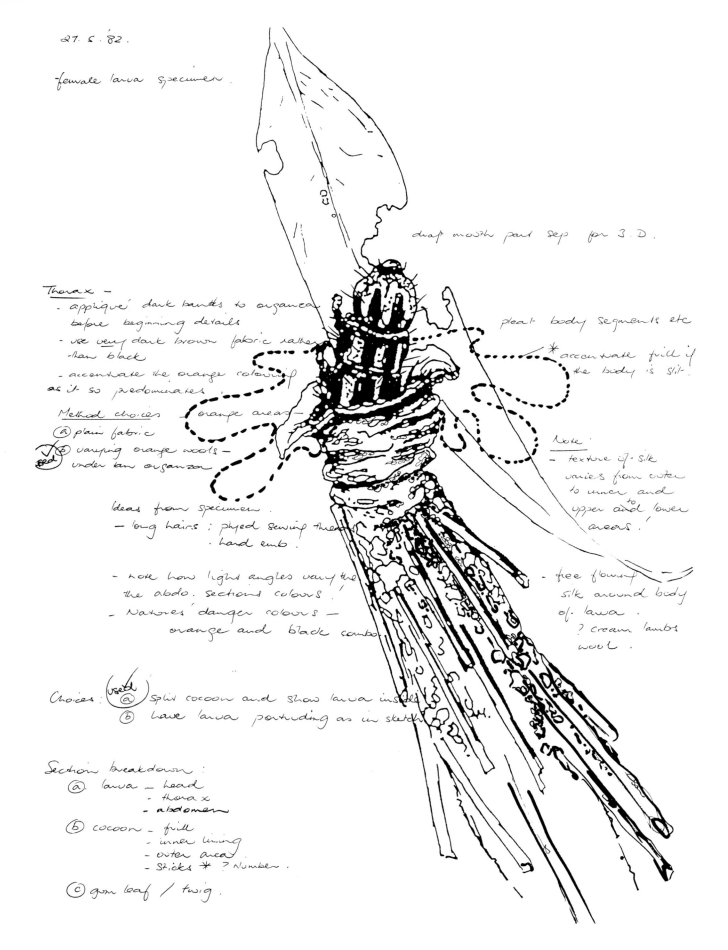

27. 5. '82.

female larva specimen.

draft mouth part sep. for 3.D.

Thorax –
- appliqué dark bands to organza before beginning details
- use very dark brown fabric rather than black
- accentuate the orange colouring as it so predominates

Method choices — orange areas —
ⓐ plain fabric
ⓑ varying orange wools — under tan organza ✓ used

Ideas from specimen.
– long hairs: dyed sewing thread. hand emb.

– note how light angles vary the abdo. sections colours.
– Natures' danger colours — orange and black combo

Choices: ⓐ used Split cocoon and show larva inside
ⓑ have larva protruding as in sketch.

Section breakdown:
ⓐ. larva – head
– thorax
– abdomen
ⓑ cocoon – frill
– inner lining
– outer area.
– sticks * ? Number.
ⓒ gum leaf / twig.

pleat body segments etc

* accentuate frill if the body is slit.

Note:
– texture of silk varies from outer to inner and upper to and lower areas.

– free flowing silk around body of larva.
? cream lambs wool.

Working sketch for No. 27, *Case Moth Cocoons.*

8

their colour, texture, durability, credibility and aesthetic appeal. These fabrics are then meticulously painted and stitched to enhance the tactile quality that is unique to textiles. For example, sheer silk stockings basically resemble the wings of many insects but with appropriate embellishment they can be made to mimic a particular species quite remarkably. Similarly, a piece of dull green wool can be transformed into a leaf, a frog, a moth wing or a grasshopper. Each type of fabric has its individual inspiration for me. I am an avid collector of all sorts of materials, whether new, pre-loved or recycled. A room in my home is devoted to their storage in colour-graded compartments, and I treasure my fabric collection.

Pattern drafting is an exacting stage in all my works. I draft tissue-paper patterns from the completed full-scale pencil-on-paper design layout. Angles have to be precisely drafted to suit the size and shape of the relief areas. This is rather like drafting darts in a dress to fit the female form. The designs for sculptural textiles often need to be broken down into many separate sections, as in *Slate Pencil Sea Urchin* and *Fallen Red Gum Log*. Also, because of the size limitations imposed by the arm of the sewing machine, all my wall designs are divided into small workable areas. Large works, such as *Freedom* and *Fantail Rhapsody*, are made up of several hundred pieces of fabric. Each small part is individually stitched before being attached to the backing fabric, a process rather like working on a giant jig-saw puzzle. Even with extensive forward planning, areas often have to be remade, their colours or textures toned up or down to modify the effect. Other pieces may be scrapped altogether. While these small sections are only pinned or tacked together, there is a great deal of improvisation and alteration, such as adjusting angles, particularly in relief areas. A few degrees can make an enormous difference to the balance, design flow, optical impression and shadows cast. Even when taking great care, there are often days when I seem to be doing more unpicking than sewing.

The sewing is only the last of many stages in a work. It is the culmination of sometimes weeks of planning, with an infinite number of decisions made daily that will all affect the end product. Fine details, such as the expression of an eye or the stamens of flowers, are sewn by hand. Sculptural forms particularly require a lot of hand sewing to avoid flattening their outer shape. This is a slow, laborious job but well worth the effort.

Machine embroidery involves only four variations of the basic lock stitch: straight stitch, zig-zag, stitches with more thread showing on the front of the fabric, or those with more showing on the back. When these are combined with different stitch lengths, widths, needles, feet, threads and fabrics the various possibilities are endless. Each work featured in this book has been stitched on normal household sewing machines – Husqvarna Class 20, and models 6570, 6370, 990 and 1100.

I take pride in the neatness of completed work so all thread ends are tied off at the back of the canvas or inside the relief structure to achieve a flat, strong, secure and tidy finish. Where possible they are also 'invisibly' embroidered back into the fabric. Some large works have countless thousands of ends to tie and I deal with them on a daily basis. Steam ironing the individual parts, as well as the total canvas, is also a constant chore.

The techniques I use include machine embroidery, painting, dyeing, appliqué, trapunto, quilting, pleating, moulding, sculpting, felting, hand embroidery, beading, spinning, weaving, plying, stiffening and wiring – in a limitless number of combinations.

My major commissioners and patrons deserve a mention. They have allowed me artistic, financial and emotional freedom within the constraints of a sound brief. They have also allowed me to exhibit their commissions prior to installation in their home environment. I acknowledge their large contribution to my artistic growth and development, and thank them sincerely.

Textile art and Australian wildlife have become my hobby, profession and addiction.

TEXTILE WORKS

I
WHITE-FACED HERON

[1978]

Flat embroidered wall panel
155 × 115 cm
Sale Regional Arts Centre

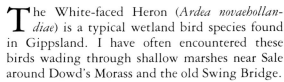

The White-faced Heron (*Ardea novaehollandiae*) is a typical wetland bird species found in Gippsland. I have often encountered these birds wading through shallow marshes near Sale around Dowd's Morass and the old Swing Bridge.

The panel portrays the graceful White-faced Heron startled and off balance after being disturbed while feeding. I have tried to portray its elegance of wing, neck and legs, even under such stress.

I used tones of blue, grey, white and tan – one of my favourite colour combinations. The calm watery surface of the wetlands and the hazy trees on the horizon are depicted using fine silk organza sewn directly onto the backing fabric.

In 1978 I had only just discovered the effects of silk organza, and loved the way it could be used to enhance perspective and distance by allowing the underlying fabric to slightly show through. By using one, two or three layers of silk organza, totally different colour tones, images and density can be achieved.

This is an early work, sewn before I began to use semi-relief techniques. The feathers have a small amount of padding behind the breast area, but they mostly rely on multilayering and different fabrics for the feathery textured effect.

White-faced Heron was the first work I sold to a regional or State gallery. Since then the Sale Regional Arts Centre, with assistance from the Crafts Board of the Australia Council, has acquired eight major textiles, seven sewing samplers and several works on paper.

13

2

COASTAL BANKSIA

[1978]

Low-relief wall panel
85 × 112 cm
Private collection

*C*oastal Banksia is typical of my early works, with its strong central subject and a large area of balancing empty space. To me, space in a work is just as powerful as embroidered detail and so requires equal attention in the design stage.

This work was a breakthrough in my experiments with semi-relief textiles. My previous works in appliqué and machine embroidery were traditional in technique, with the cut fabric edges sewn in satin or zig-zag stitch, like making a stained-glass window in textiles. They were also

almost flat. Here I wanted to portray the distinctive silver colour of the underside of the banksia leaf (*Banksia integrifolia*). I found that by sewing two different colours of fabric together I was able to mould and curl the leaf to reveal the underside and achieve a more realistic appearance. This low-relief 'sculpting' was to be explored extensively in my later works.

In this design satin stitch remains the predominant means of attaching fabric to fabric and eliminating frayable edges. It also includes my first experiments in free-sewing, using the sewing machine like a drawing pencil. These linear areas caused some controversy when *Coastal Banksia* was first exhibited. Comments such as 'Why didn't you finish the work?' and 'Drawing on fabric is not acceptable in embroidery' were commonplace. I wanted to avoid dense, stark appliqué and with mere suggestions of forms create an illusion of distance and perspective.

With this free-sewing I have complete control over the movement of the fabric as well as the machine's speed, and the placement, length and direction of the stitches. I ease off the pressure on the presser foot, or lower the feed dogs, to make an unobstructed space for the fabric; adjust the stitch length to small (0.5–1 mm) and the thread tension according to the thickness of the fabric; put the presser foot lever down and sew reasonably fast. As the fabric can only go where I want it to while the needle is out of the fabric, the faster I sew, the faster I can move the fabric at will without breaking the needle. I don't use a hoop; instead my fingers and palms keep the fabric taut and flat. A see-through plastic foot filed down to the bare essentials allows a better view of the sewing area.

Coastal Banksia has three visual levels: a few fine stitched lines of free-sewing to suggest distant background; flat appliqué and machine embroidery; and low-relief leaves.

The choice of fabrics was all-important: the banksia-nut base is of textured bouclé wool; the opened nuts themselves are of wool, felt and silk; and the leaves are wool with silver velvet underlining.

Coastal Banksia won the Family Circle/Coats Patons Craft Award in December 1978. It was the first competition I had entered and the boost to my motivation and confidence was immense.

3
EASTERN WATER DRAGON

[1979]

Low-relief wall panel
117 × 132 × 6 (relief) cm
Private collection

My first face-to-face encounter with an Eastern Water Dragon (*Physignathus howittii*) was in a secluded spot at The Quarries along the Freestone Creek at Briagolong in Gippsland. Its colour markings provided exquisite camouflage among the rocks, branches and water. Since then I have often seen them while canoeing our waterways and have sometimes been quite startled by their sudden movement. They like basking on overhanging tree branches and then dramatically splashing into the water when they are disturbed. Their fearless reptilian expression reminds me of huge fairytale dragons, and they invoke in me a sense of history, and of evolution.

I designed this portrayal of the Eastern Water Dragon to be larger than life-size and as big as was possible to execute on a normal dressmaking sewing machine. It is also an example of my early experiments in drafting for sharp relief angles, padding from behind and quilting. The lizard's head was designed, drafted, cut and stitched in nine separate sections to achieve the required shapes and angles, such as the bulging eye, recessed nostril, indented jaw-line and puffed-out cheeks.

Only unpatterned coloured fabrics were used as I preferred to create the textural and scale variations on the skin with stitches. The scales were free-sewn in roughly circular patterns, varying only in colour tones, size and amounts of stitching.

The wall panel portrays the quiet confidence and seeming arrogance of the Eastern Water Dragon. Its size, the tilt of its head, the sardonic smile, the unblinking eye and poised 'ready to pounce' look all add to its awesomeness. The work prompts amazing reactions from the public, particularly from young children, who often find it too frightening to look at!

4
THE MORASS – SALE
[1979]

Four low-relief wall panels
103 × 100 cm each
Private collection

The Morass – Sale was my first private commission. The shape and size (the four panels are 4.5 metres wide when hung together) and subject matter were specifically designed for a very long lounge room that overlooked a vast and magnificent area of wetlands on the outskirts of Sale. The main interior colours of the house are repeated throughout the work – the earthy browns of the brick walls, the greens and yellows of the upholstery and cushions, and the tans of antique furniture and polished wood.

The panels highlight some of the varieties of flora and fauna found in that wetland environment, including dragonflies and damselflies, shield beetles, pelicans, a Reed Warbler family and nest, frogs, carp, a yabby and a snail, River Red Gum blossoms and leaves, native bees and water-reeds. The distant tree line suggests the wattles and gums on the far side of the morass. It is an overcast and foggy morning, yet the birds and insects are already busy in their daily routine. The whole work gives a relaxed view of nature's purposeful activity.

Each panel leads to the other in a two-way directional flow. I used the long water-grasses to link the four brown frames and to gently direct the eye from panel to panel. The work is best seen first from a distance for an overview of its environmental setting and atmosphere, then examined more closely for the fine details and individual components.

In *The Morass – Sale* I employed all my sewing skills of the time, including silk layering, free-sewing in simple lines, quilting, padding, drafting patterns for the angles of the relief work and constructing these sections, and appliqué. This fibre collage remains one of my favourite works.

COSTUMES

During 1979–80 I was at a crossroad in textile experimentation. The major decision was whether to continue producing works for the wall or to diversify into clothes.

I had already made two items of clothing for 'Crafts

in Gear 1979' (a regional then State and national exhibition), both of which were purchased on exhibition. Orders were flooding in for ties, jackets and hats. Decorative clothing was certainly popular and relatively easy to sell.

I decided to continue working with non-functional textiles, though the choice was neither easy nor clear. I have, however, made at least one item of clothing per year, purely for the pleasure of doing so.

Costumes

5
BUSH JACKET
[1979]

Size 18
National Gallery of Victoria

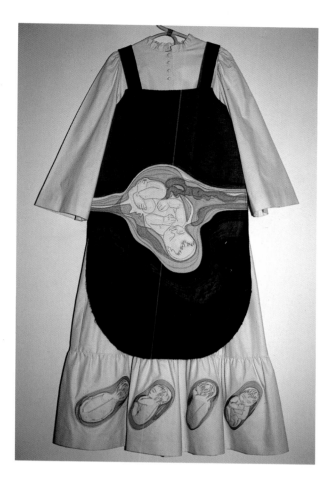

Long before I made this jacket I had become acutely aware of the Australian landscape and its importance to me – artistically and emotionally. On field trips I wore clothes that harmonised with my surroundings. The colours of the jacket reflect the subtle earthy brown tones of this sunburnt country.

The woven raw-silk jacket is decorated with appliqué and machine embroidery depicting a honeyeater family on the front. The pocket has become the nest containing three young, the buttons are plastic-sealed real Southern Blue Gum nuts, and the back shows two frogs chasing each other up a twig. The jacket is quilted in gum-leaf and reed-grass shapes. The lining is of the same raw silk.

Costumes

6

MATERNITY DRESS
[1979]

Size 16
National Gallery, Canberra

This is a two-piece maternity outfit designed to celebrate the International Year of the Child in 1979.

Around the hemline of the full-length cream calico dress are eight unborn babies in various stages of development. All the internal seams of the dress are bound with cream lace.

The pinafore is made of navy blue wool with silk and mohair appliquéd in shades of green, blue-grey, brown and cream. The front shows the full-term baby – just where it would be lying inside its mother. The back shows a portrait of the parents.

ABOVE Front view of Maternity Dress.
BELOW Back view of Maternity Dress.
OPPOSITE Bush Jacket.

7
DRAGONFLY CAPE
[1981]

Size 16
Private collection

The *Dragonfly Cape* is the outer covering of a four-piece outfit that includes the *Lacewing Vest*, *Moth Skirt* and *Beetle Slip*. It is a whimsical work, designed to envelop the human female form in insects – the study of insects being one of my lasting passions.

The base fabric is raw, hand-spun cotton, and the insect embellishments are in silk, wool, silk stockings, fur, dacron and machine embroidery threads.

Costumes

8

LACEWING VEST

[1981]

Size 12
Private collection
See Dragonfly Cape *notes*

9
BUTTERFLY TIES
{1981}

Private collection

These two ties were made for my husband and father-in-law to wear with their grey suits to my exhibition at the National Gallery of Victoria in 1981. Similar shades of grey and blue were used, in differing proportions, to make the ties matching yet individual.

10
FISHERMAN'S TIE
{1989}

Private collection

This tie shows a colourful salmon leaping for the fly and hook. It is made of black leatherette, hand-painted silk and embroidery threads. It was commissioned for an enthusiastic fisherman friend's birthday.

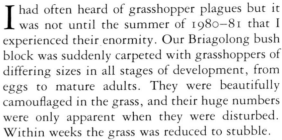

II
GRASSHOPPERS
[1980]

Two low-relief wall panels
105 × 105 cm each
Queensland Art Gallery

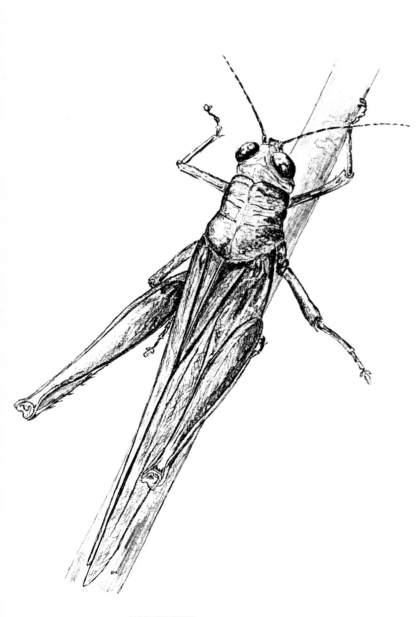

I had often heard of grasshopper plagues but it was not until the summer of 1980–81 that I experienced their enormity. Our Briagolong bush block was suddenly carpeted with grasshoppers of differing sizes in all stages of development, from eggs to mature adults. They were beautifully camouflaged in the grass, and their huge numbers were only apparent when they were disturbed. Within weeks the grass was reduced to stubble.

A friend living in Brisbane then sent me specimens of Queensland grasshoppers (*Austracris guttulosa*). I was so impressed by their beauty and size – they were three times the size of my largest local specimen – that I began designing *Grasshoppers*. Ironically, the completed panels were purchased by the Queensland Art Gallery. It seemed as if the grasshoppers were going home.

In these textile panels I have depicted four huge, short-horned grasshoppers eating, flying and camouflaged in their grassland habitat. Like the specimens I worked with, they have a distinctively arrogant and prehistoric air, and their many-faceted eyes seem to stare blindly. The choice of fabric for the eyes was very important for the credibility of the portrayal. My father-in-law kindly relinquished an old yellow silk tie as its colour, texture and weave remarkably resembled the eyes of live grasshoppers.

The work was made in two parts for easier handling during the sewing stages.

An audiovisual presentation on the preliminary drawings, sketches, final layout designs and construction is included in the Queensland Art Gallery's collection.

Grasshoppers, detail.

No. 11, *Grasshoppers*, two low-relief wall panels.

I 2
FROGS
[1980]

High-relief wall sculpture
131 × 95 × 8 (relief) cm
Hoechst Australia, Melbourne

I have always had an affection for frogs. Although they are reptilian, they seem to display human characteristics and movements. This wall sculpture portrays the agility and acrobatic skills of a male frog (*Litoria aurea*) in his determination to reach his mate. Whether she will receive him or not is another matter, for she is poised, ready to jump. Over the past ten years I have made several different frog panels of which this work is the largest. It was certainly a milestone in my career and development.

Frogs received the inaugural Hoechst Textile Award at the official opening of the Centenary Celebration Exhibition, 'Australian Crafts 1980', at the Meat Market Craft Centre in Melbourne.

It is the first work in which I used textile paint. It is also an early example of mixed high and low-relief textile areas on a flat background.

The background fabric is raw hand-woven cotton. Some reeds are only stitched, some are painted using a stencil, while others are of fine silk organza or heavy woven woollen fabric. They give the illusion of being on different perspective planes and so help create a more three-dimensional appearance.

13
DRAGONFLIES
[1980]

Low-relief wall panel
122 × 122 cm
Sale Regional Arts Centre

These beautiful, fast flyers are a common sight over the wetlands, rivers and creeks of East Gippsland in summer. I first witnessed dragonfly eclosion (the final stage of metamorphosis when the fully developed adult insect emerges or 'hatches' from its larva or nymphal skin) at the lakeside property of Pat and Charles McCubbin in Longford, Victoria. On that sunny day I saw hundreds of drab brown dragonfly nymphs laboriously crawl out of the water, clinging to any available dry surface, and begin the slow drying-out phase. With that achieved, their backs split down the centre. The emergence of the powder-blue males with their sparkling wings was simply breathtaking.

Dragonflies is a soft and subtly toned blue, green and cream textile. It captures two male dragonflies (*Orthetrum caledonicum*) in mid-flight, engaged in a graceful airborne battle to establish their territory over a dandelion seed-head. Their aggression is portrayed in their leg actions and head angles. One is hunched down, while the other is braced for striking and biting. An illusion of movement is created by their shimmery, rippled and semi-relief wings, together with the circular bands of painted sunlight behind them.

The dandelion seed-head is the dominant territorial marker. Its top section is silk organza quilted over different shades of dyed raw wool, while the seeds are hand embroidered.

14

CUP MOTHS

[1980]

High-relief wall sculpture
134 × 102 × 10 (relief) cm
Private collection

Cup Moths features mature moths (*Doratifera vulnerans*), closed cocoons, or 'cups' as they are commonly called, and an empty cocoon with its old pupal case protruding from the lid.

In the wild, cup moth cocoons are so well camouflaged in shape, texture and colour that many people believe them to be gum nuts. This work was an exercise in camouflage and shows the important relationship between the subject and its food plant environment. Shapes and colours are repeated within the moths' wings and the leaves, using stitches, paint and relief sculpting.

To achieve the characteristic fluffiness of moths I made their heads, thoraxes and abdomens from soft brown rabbit fur, hand quilted into segments and padded to raise the level of these parts even further.

The gum leaves were worked in a number of techniques that suited the chosen fabrics and each leaf's placement in the design. The dark green leaves were made from two layers of thick wool from an old army jacket. Their edges were satin stitched together in matching green thread and their surface was embroidered with veins. The thickness of the wool and the density of the stitching enabled me to achieve an almost rigid leaf that would retain its semi-relief shape. The paler leaves were made of linen, backed with silk organza, that was soft enough to reverse seam (bag out or turn right side out) into long, thin, pointed leaves. Reversed seams create an unfrayable edge and this is my basic technique for appliqué and machine embroidery. Two layers of cut fabric are stitched around the edges on the wrong side, leaving a small hole, then the layers are turned right side out through the hole so that all raw edges are concealed inside. The hole is then closed by hand sewing. A section that is 'self-reversed' has identical fabric for both layers.

To turn the fabric inside out I use a large, curved bagging needle with the point filed off to avoid poking holes in the seams. The curves of the leaves and their eaten-out holes require careful trimming of surplus fabric and precise cutting of notches to prevent lumps, fraying edges or distortion of the shape.

The illusion of distant leaves on the backing cotton was achieved by using paper stencils and spraying them with diluted paint from an insect spray gun.

In *Cup Moths* the leaves all have a slightly windswept look as though a gentle breeze has lifted their tips. I deliberately set out to suggest that 'something has been here before', with the many eaten-out holes in the leaves. When the larvae of cup moths, sawflies or case moths are at large, it is very difficult to find a perfect gum leaf. Since this work was first exhibited in 1980, eaten-out sections of leaves have become one of my trademarks.

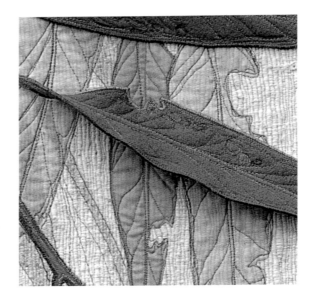

15
CUP MOTH LARVA
[1980–89]

Freestanding sculpture
61 × 17 × 17 (height) cm
Private collection

I have often set myself the challenging task of portraying 'unlovable' species in order to emphasise their attractiveness, individuality and variety. By greatly increasing their size, and hence their visual impact on man, I have been able to communicate intricate details of their beauty and interest. Over the years this technique has received a remarkable response from the public with comments such as, 'I saw one of these grubs, and you're right – they are incredible!' or 'I'd have squashed it if I hadn't seen your work'.

This textile was inspired by my husband's misfortune when two cup moth larvae (*Doratifera vulnerans*) dropped inside his shirt while he was pruning our eucalypts. Their hairy tufts left long tram-track welts on his back and arms, forcing me to have a good long look at the caterpillars. Immediately, perhaps instinctively, I knew they would be the subject of a future work.

Some months later, when the nearly completed textile caterpillar was sitting on the studio stairs, our seven-year-old son, Peter, suddenly screamed, 'There's a monster one of those things that got Dad on your stairs, Mum!'. He took quite a lot of pacifying.

The *Cup Moth Larva* sculpture was originally designed to sit in front of the main wall work *Cup Moths*. It was attached to a large fabric roll. In 1989 I removed the caterpillar and leaf from its fabric backing and reshaped it as a freestanding sculpture.

In contrast to the adult moths, cup moth larvae are brilliantly coloured on their back 'saddle'. In the sculpture I have minutely explored the different surface qualities of body hair, stinging bunches, textured saddle and rubbery skin, using a variety of materials including fur, wool, silk and wire.

16
SAWFLIES
[1980]

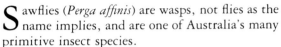

High-relief wall sculpture
130 × 95 × 10 (relief) cm
Private collection

Sawflies (*Perga affinis*) are wasps, not flies as the name implies, and are one of Australia's many primitive insect species.

Sawflies was the first work in which I used the effect of 'inside looking out', almost like a diorama. This setting created an atmosphere and mood that I was to use again many years later in *Fabric Fantasy*. Here the underground impression shows the brilliant green, tan and yellow sawflies hatching from their motley cocoons and heading straight for daylight.

What still appeals to me in this work is its seemingly simple design. At the time, however, it was the most complex work I had tackled. More hours were spent in field work, drawing, designing, composition, and colour selection than the total number spent in sewing. That is not unusual today, but in 1980 the complexity of this work was almost overwhelming. Time and time again it was set aside while I tried to resolve interplaying areas of open space, close detail, proportions and the general underground rounded-tunnel effect.

Over two years I had nurtured and 'hatched' hundreds of sawflies – collecting the caterpillars (larvae) in boxes of soil as they descended from the trees to pupate. Glass partitions in the soil allowed me to observe their construction of the densely clustered silk-and-soil cocoons and, months later, their noisy emergence as adult sawflies. Many sketches of their determined scramble to the light gave me the empathy to give this work credibility from a human view. Mentally I placed myself in their position underground, fresh with the instinct for reproduction and new life, then seeking daylight and escape!

The warp and weft of the woollen backing fabric was unravelled and reapplied to the surface by machine to create the brown colour tones of the tunnel. The circular hole shape is repeated also in the tree roots, cocoon openings and front legs of the wasps. Colour was used carefully and selectively, and limited to tones of green, brown and yellow that were repeated in the painted scene, with a splash of cream for brightness.

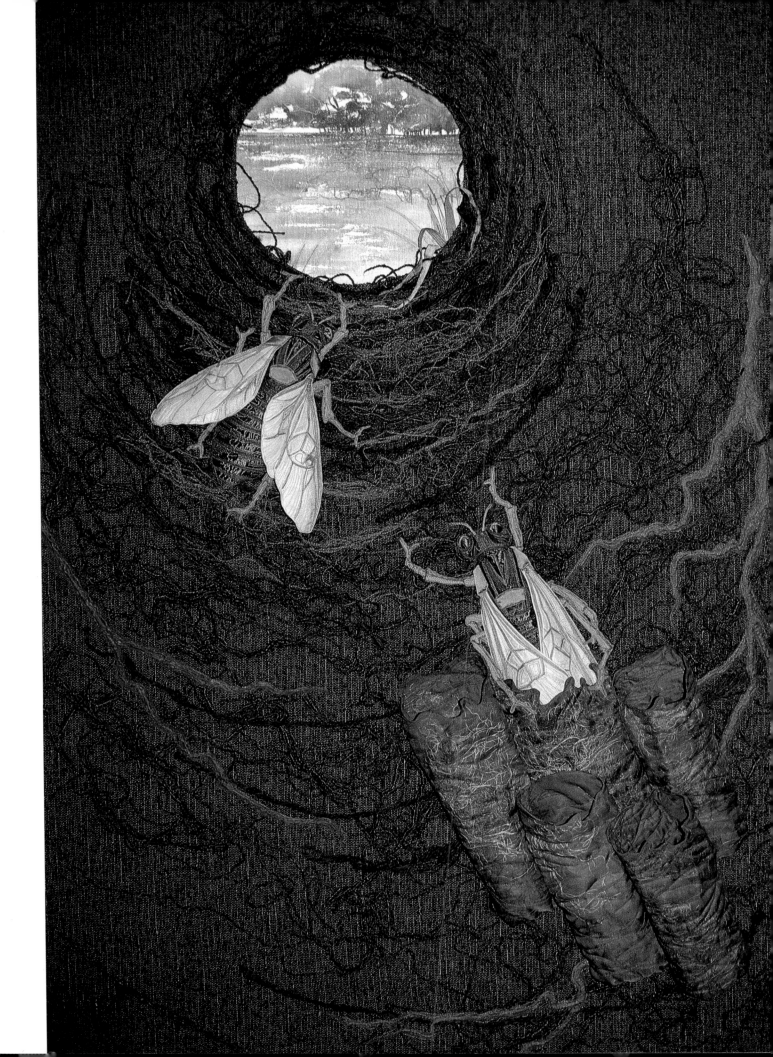

17
SUPERB BLUE WRENS
[1981]

Low-relief wall panel
120 × 140 × 5 (relief) cm
Sale Regional Arts Centre

My garden in Sale has been the home of a Superb Blue Wren family (*Malurus cyaneus*) for ten years. I have found them readily attracted with morsels of cheese or breadcrumbs, yet astute enough to remain completely 'wild'. The sight and sounds of their hunting antics and acrobatics never fail to cheer me.

Superb Blue Wrens shows a hungry, demanding and full-of-action juvenile wren just after it has ventured out of the nest. The colourful adult male offers it a succulent grasshopper.

Their textile 'environment' is designed to suggest low scrub, with messy foliage, bracken, twigs and dead leaves in stitches and appliqué, and paint used for shadows.

My main intention was to capture the expression and animation of the young bird as it was demanding to be fed. Its unbalanced stance, with wings flapping to maintain a hold, tail splayed unnaturally wide and mouth agape, all say 'Feed me now!'. In contrast, the blue male stands serenely, taking his time. I have often wanted to play a sound recording with this work so that others could experience the volume of noise such a small bird can produce.

Up to seven layers of fine silk organza, and intricate embroidery, were used to achieve the desired feather effects of hard quills, soft down, dark shadows, highlights and colour gradings in this work.

An audiovisual presentation on the preliminary drawings, sketches, layouts, sewing samples and construction is included in the Sale Regional Arts Centre's collection.

18
CHRISTMAS BEETLES
[1981]

High-relief wall sculpture with relief sections
extending beyond the frame
150 × 125 × 8 (relief) cm
Private collection

*C*hristmas Beetles is one of my environmental statement works depicting the devastation caused by indiscriminate clearing of our native forests for pasture. Sadly, it is only quite recently that the importance of leaving stands of trees around farmland has been understood.

Alfred William Howitt (1830–1908), an early Gippsland naturalist, predicted in the late 1800s the destruction these beetles (*Anoplognathus* sp.) would cause as a result of extensive land clearing for pasture or crops. The cycle is as follows. Early Gippsland farmers removed most of the Red Gum forests for pasture land. The larvae of the Christmas Beetle feed on plant roots, and pasture paddocks enhance their survival. Once they develop into winged adult beetles they feed on eucalyptus leaves. Over recent years we have had plague proportions of beetles defoliating the few remaining ancient trees and causing their death. So now we have even fewer trees and this is implicated in pasture salination problems.

The textile suggests the beetles' ferocious nocturnal appetites with bare branches and eaten-out holes in the few remaining leaves. More beetles are flying in, indicating imminent defoliation. Procreation is also in progress – the devastating cycle continues. Eaten leaves hang beyond the frame, drooping downward, sinking to earth and death. This was the first time I had used space beyond the frame. I had often wanted to make a work even larger than originally designed and this was a way to do so without having to add joins to the background fabric. I also enjoy not being constricted within a frame. Perhaps that is what appeals to me about so many Art Nouveau designs.

19
THE POTTER WASP I
[1981]

High-relief wall sculpture
142 × 102 × 12 (relief) cm
Private collection

An airborne potter wasp (*Eumenes* sp.) is struggling to carry a large daub of mud to seal off her pot, which contains a paralysed grub and her newly laid egg. I had keenly observed these wasps in action over several seasons. It took many hundreds of flights to make the pots, and I was amazed to see the weight a wasp could carry in food and mud. Once again I have depicted a rather 'unlovable' insect but feel that its gory survival behaviour and success deserve to be admired.

Like many of my previous works, the composition has a strong central design, a limited colour range, repeated shapes and an extensive use of open space to balance dense detail.

Many rough and many detailed sketches were made of the female wasp struggling under the burden of heavy daubs of mud. Days were spent on the design layout, moving portable cutouts of wasps (separate body segments, wings, head and legs) and cocoons a smidgin here or a hairsbreadth there. A hand mirror was used to see the work in reverse to help correct my familiarity with the drawings and my right-eye dominance.

The upward thrust of the various cocoons and the dominant right to left angles within the design were intended to emphasise the wasp's struggle to fly. The angles of her legs and abdomen and the tilt of her head all help to create the feeling of a heavy burden.

Twenty-eight cocoons are depicted in a variety of techniques ranging from simple line-stitching, painting and back padding to low and high relief sculpting.

This work also illustrates the power of a frame. It is mounted on two levels: the plane of the inner canvas is raised by 1 centimetre. This double framing creates an empty space around the central design to give it more strength and prominence.

20

THE POTTER WASP II
[1982]

Freestanding sculpture
18 × 16 × 19 (height) cm
Sale Regional Arts Centre

Afemale wasp (*Eumenes* sp.) is shown tensed and struggling to place a paralysed grub inside a completed pot. Her delicate freestanding wings are of four layers of fabric – glittery silk stockings, veil netting, cream silk and a heavy iron-on backing.

The textile mud pots, made from overlaid and colour-graded silks, wools and sewing-thread off-cuts, are arranged around the cylinder 'drainpipe' and are depicted in various stages of construction. Balance and perspective are largely created by the pots: they are graded in size; some are only painted, others lightly stitched, while the dominant forms are either quilted, stuffed, or are totally in relief.

Each sculpted pot began as an embroidered square of fabric with a central self-reversed hole. The pots were shaped by manipulating the fabric into darts, tucks and pleats while hand sewing together the surplus folds bunched up inside them. The quantity and thickness of the internal fabric gives them their self-supporting solidity.

The wasp is similar in design to the flat 'camouflaged among the pots' wasp in *Potter Wasp I*, only here she is more colourful, textured and in relief.

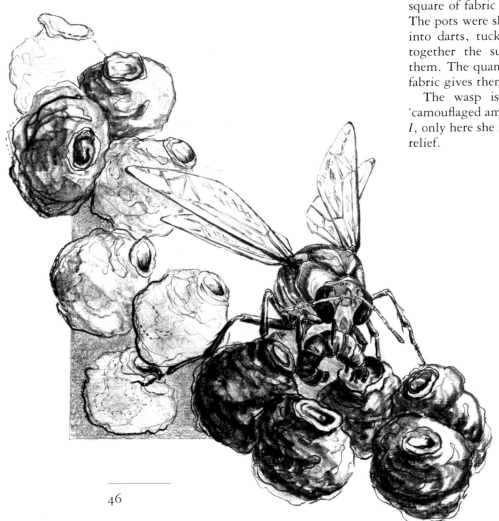

21
THE OLD LADY MOTH
[1981]

Freestanding tactile sculpture
103 × 60 × 20 (height) cm
Private collection

I have always loved handling fabrics and enjoyed the variations in textures and surfaces. At previous exhibitions I had difficulty preventing people from touching my works – 'Just checking to feel if it really is fabric' was a common response.

So *The Old Lady Moth* was specifically designed to be handled by the public at my exhibition at the National Gallery of Victoria, 'Environmental Textiles', in 1981 – hence the careful choice of durable fabrics and a dark-coloured insect. The moth (*Dasypodia selenophora*), the leaves and the backing fabrics all incorporated a cross-section of fabrics and techniques used in other works at that exhibition, and thus gave the public a chance to handle and feel the textures and stitching effects. The catalogue read: 'Do explore the moth, its wings and its body. Find its bald spot and examine the differences in textures. Note the proboscis, which when at rest, is coiled under the head, like a clock spring'. This work became a very popular component of the exhibition, particularly with children.

Although it is a night moth, the Old Lady Moth has mostly caught my eye in the daytime, crippled and fluttering pathetically to avoid the sunshine. In September 1981 large numbers were found in Sale, battered and flight-weary, in carports, verandahs and sheds.

In this sculpture the moth's body is made of rabbit fur, and the antennae and legs are of plied embroidery wool. The wings are of several different colours of silk and satin, layered over each other to give subtle colour grading and tonal shading differences, and the wings' eye spots are of appliquéd silk from a recycled tie.

The leaves are made from recycled woollen overcoats and are self-reverse seamed. Two layers of identical wool were stitched along the outlined leaf shape with a small hole being left for turning the leaf inside out, so that all cut fabric and potentially fraying edges were concealed internally and seams were as unobtrusive as possible. Then they were machine embroidered for veins, highlights, blemishes and eaten-out holes.

All the machine embroidery is in straight stitch or satin stitch, using my free-sewing technique.

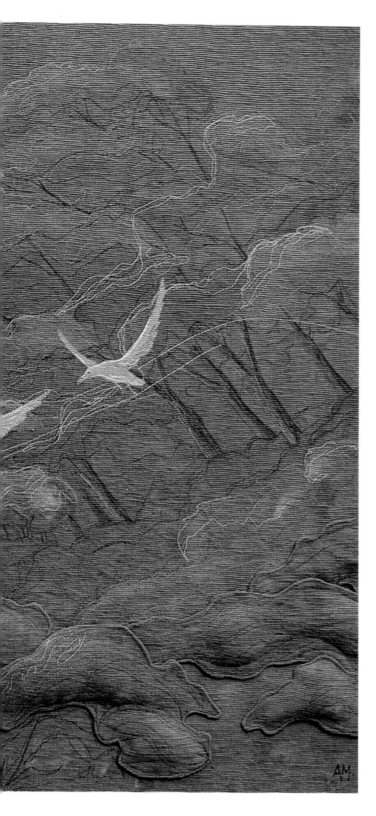

22

SQUABBLING GULLS
[1981]

Low-relief wall panel
95 × 128 × 5 (relief) cm
Private collection

Seagulls are gregarious, aggressive and noisy scavengers. Many of my early Australian childhood memories include seagulls, dozens of seagulls, and all of them my friends. My father was a keen fisherman and the gull colonies at Waratah Bay, near Wilsons Promontory, gave me companionship and hours of pleasure. I remember sitting very still, gently feeding them and gaining their confidence so completely that they would land on my legs, arms and head.

About thirty years later I specifically designed this work for my parents' new home. In preparation, I went to Lake Guthridge in Sale to recapture my feelings for seagulls. The birds did not fail me. Within hours I had them sitting all over me again.

The design features two gulls (*Larus novaehollandiae*) squabbling in an airborne battle over a potato cake. Others are in hot pursuit. The windswept trees, the undergrowth on the banks and the cream-stitched flight-lines all lead to the gulls. A dark brown woven backing fabric and the limited use of colours highlight the pale gulls.

The flight-lines were included to add directional flow and give more squabbling animation to the total design. These lines stemmed from the original pencil-on-paper drawings when I was sketching out perspective and eye-flow directional pulls within the composition.

Reproducing the gulls' cream-on-white and white-on-white colouration in machine embroidery was challenging. Over twenty different shades of white, cream and brown were used to subtly define the feathers' outlines and their underlying shadows. I wanted to retain a crisp whiteness in the overall visual impression and the sharply contrasting dark background fabric helped achieve this.

The feather-fall on the underwing of the dominant gull was quite a trial too. Gulls do not remain still for long with their wings up in the air. Finally I temporarily captured one, drew the underwing feather patterns and then released the bird. He was no worse for the experience and readily came back for more food.

No. 22, *Squabbling Gulls*, details.

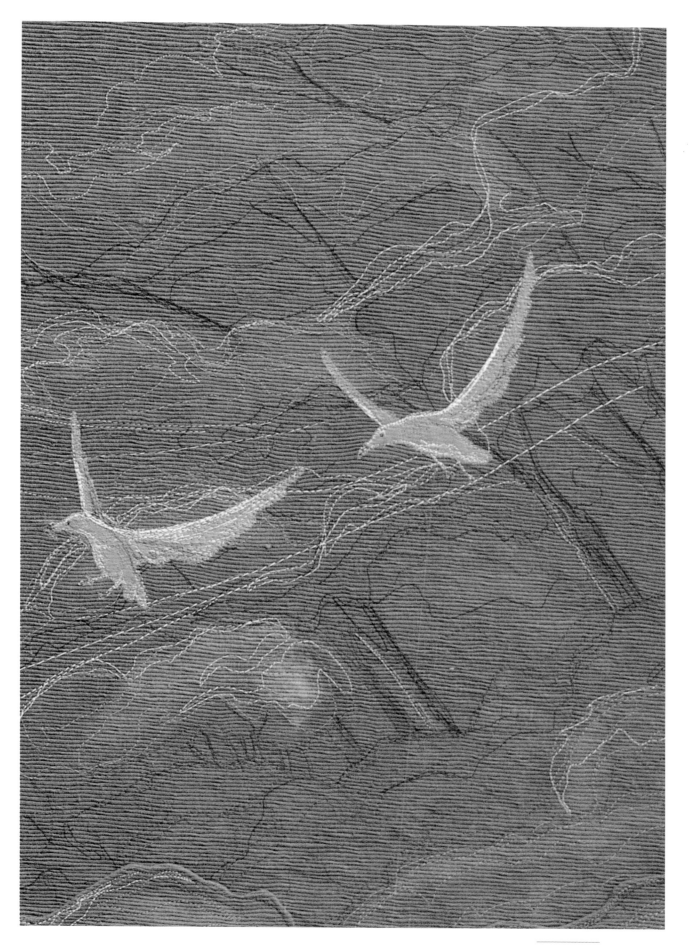

23
PINK EMPEROR GUM
MOTH I
[1982]

Freestanding sculpture
60 × 50 × 13 (height) cm
Ararat Gallery

Learning about Australia's vast and varied insect species is probably my favourite spare-time occupation and I shall never forget watching my first Emperor Gum Moth (*Opodiphthera eucalypti*) emerge from its cocoon. It was extraordinarily beautiful. Since then I have seen dozens hatch, in colours varying from yellow, tan, brown, grey and beige to pink.

I had made a number of moth and cocoon related works over the years and this was the first sculpture. It portrays the sunset's glow on the brilliant pink colours of the newly emerged male Emperor Gum Moth. His broad wings are outspread and fully pumped up. The colourful eye spots on the rear wings can barely be seen as he clings to the cocoon for the duration of the wing-drying process.

The whole work is supported internally by covered millinery wire that may be bent or angled as desired. The cocoon and branch are made of hundreds of coloured threads underneath pink and brown organza that is then machined and sculpted into shape. The wings are of about six layers of silk organza, a multilayering that gives a moiré effect. The body is of rabbit fur and the antennae are emu feathers.

Freestanding textile sculptures can be viewed from all angles, including the bottom. Consequently the neatness of finish is important to me. All my sewing-thread ends are triple-knotted and invisibly darned away between the layers of fabric so that they remain securely hidden. The thread ends of wall panels are knotted at the back and trimmed to about a centimetre in length prior to framing.

24
PINK EMPEROR GUM MOTH II
[1982]

Low-relief wall panel
85 × 130 × 5 (relief) cm
Private collection

The moths (*Opodiphthera eucalypti*) and the cocoon in *Pink Emperor Gum Moth II* were made in the same way as in the freestanding sculpture *Pink Emperor Gum Moth I*.

This work is an example of how the grading of limited colours helps create the impression of dominance and recession in perspective. Only coordinating tones of pink, green and brown have been stitched on the painted and woven backing fabric. Low and high-relief areas interplay in the design also by creating texture and casting shadows.

One moth is portrayed freshly emerged from her cocoon with wings outspread in the drying process. By revealing the large and brilliantly coloured eye spots on the lower wings she hopes to scare off any potential attackers while she is in this vulnerable stage of her metamorphosis. A paler, airborne moth is leaving the scene.

The eucalypt branch, with its attached cocoon, has fallen into the undergrowth among the Pink Beard Heath (*Leucopogon ericoides*). This heath was made by unravelling the ends of carpet wool and then attaching the tiny fluffy pieces to the surface of the background fabric with free-sewing. Many different embossed effects can be achieved with this method of attaching fibres to fabric – for example, the gum blossoms in *The Morass – Sale*, the roots and soil in *Sawflies* and the woven nest in *Fantail Nightwatch*.

25
ABOVE THE CHANNELS
[1982]

Three low-relief wall panels
90 × 90 cm each
Private collection

The central panel depicts the Channels Gorge on the Avon River near Newry from a bird's eye view. It shows the mountainous and rocky terrain in the misty light of an early morning. Attention is focused on the intensively stitched 'window framed' area, while the plainer, unstitched surrounding canvas suggests continuing space and mystery. This panel creates the setting for the two adjoining panels.

The left panel shows a damselfly pair (*Austroagrion*) in their tandem mating flight above the water. They are portrayed in their most vulnerable state as the blue male struggles to keep height with his heavy female burden. The damselflies are also 'window framed' to suggest the limited time remaining for them; below them the water churns and fleetingly reflects their image. Two lives are about to end and another life cycle is about to begin.

In the right panel a Sacred Kingfisher (*Halcyon sancta*) has caught a male damselfly in mid-flight. He is completely free and unrestricted, able to catch his food on the wing at great speed. His action lines over the water, his shadow and flight path, together with the dancing ring of water as he clips the surface chasing his prey, were all accentuated to suggest rapid movement. His prey is the male damselfly on the left panel. So life continues.

Above the Channels was the first work in which I used heavy artist's canvas as a background fabric. I had become increasingly involved in the use of textile paints and fibre dyes with their subtle colour-toning possibilities. The washed-out appearance of the mist, hills, rocks and distant landscape was achieved by mixing textile paints to watercolour consistency and applying them to a damp canvas. The paint work was deliberately kept as simple and unobtrusive as possible to achieve the final 'out of focus' but 'continuous space' effect. Also it allowed the detailed focal area to stand out even more dominantly once the machine sewing was added.

Selected for the international travelling exhibition 'Australian Craft '83' organised by the Crafts Council of Australia, this work was exhibited in Sydney, London, Edinburgh and Hong Kong.

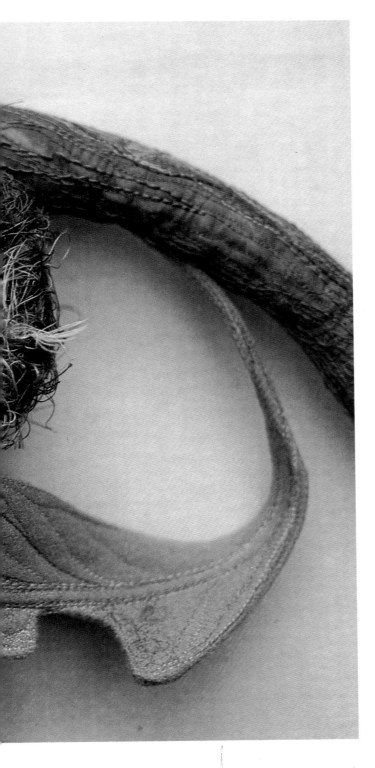

26
THE NEST
[1982]

Freestanding sculpture
90 × 40 × 10 (height) cm
Private collection

At the end of a day's sewing the studio floor is covered in thread off-cuts — thousands of them. They sometimes naturally congregate in nesty formations, providing the inspiration for a work such as this.

Another factor that inspired me to execute this sculpture was my discovery that felt could be moulded into three-dimensional forms. At a local felt-making workshop I realised that solidly compressed wool would allow me to construct a variety of shapes that would help to support my sculptures. There have been many occasions when I have been stumped over how to construct a particular shape but felting solved that problem.

The construction of nests has interested me for years. My home and studio contain about thirty different windblown nests in many shapes and sizes. All are treasures, but one in particular, made from my own hair and my studio scraps of wool, takes pride of place. Our garden Silvereyes took the hair and wool that I placed on a banksia bush to construct their delightful nest.

The Nest sculpture shows a branch, a single eucalypt leaf and a delicate little nest with three intact eggs. The nest belongs to no particular bird species — it is just an example of complexity of construction within simplicity of design. It was made by saving thread off-cuts and hand sewing them securely over a woollen felt dome. Some combed wool and real feathers were stitched into the nest to create a soft, fluffy lining. The eggs are tiny white woollen felt balls covered with three layers of silk stockings; the brown spots were hand sewn with fine embroidery thread.

The branch is of silk organza, heavily stitched to resemble the texture of bark, and filled with dacron. Inserted covered millinery wire gives it support and pliability. The leaf is of woollen fabric and is able to be turned and viewed from all angles.

27
CASE MOTH COCOONS
[1982]

Two freestanding sculptures
62 × 15 × 9 (height) cm each
Museum of Applied Arts and Sciences, Sydney

Saunder's Case Moth (*Metura elongata*) cocoons are one of nature's own textile wonders. I have always enjoyed encounters with them as they climb up our windows, leaving silken tracks that last for months, or up our west-facing brick wall to hang from the spouting and woodwork.

They have ferocious appetites and eat just about any vegetation. I have seen them feeding on broom, gum, kangaroo-paw, iris, geranium, bottlebrush and honeysuckle! There is nothing quite like watching a case moth larva devouring the leaf tissue, slitting a hole in its cocoon, biting off the leaf stalk, placing it over the cocoon hole and weaving it all together in five minutes flat. Hence the cocoon grows apace with the caterpillar body.

It was not until I learnt that the female case moth larva never leaves her cocoon that I felt inspired to portray her plight in a sculpture.

The closed cocoon shows the distinctive shape and texture of many sticks woven into the silken covering of the larva. To achieve the roughened texture, silk organza and finely woven cotton fabric were intensively embroidered on the machine, using a variety of thread colours and thread tensions. A tight bobbin tension dimpled and puckered the fabric.

The basic shape was sculpted by pleating, adding darts, padding from behind, tacking, gathering and hand sewing it into shape. The textile sticks were made of tightly packed dacron-filled tubes of fabric, all hand stitched into place. The discovery of this technique enabled me to execute the *Slate Pencil Sea Urchin* about two years later.

I have opened the cocoon to show the fully grown female larva in her lavish silk-lined bed where she will remain until her death. Her head and first three segments are nature's danger colour – brilliant orange – alternating with black. This colour variation was achieved by grading bright orange, yellow and brown wool underneath a fine layer of tan silk organza, then surface appliquéing black bands. The middle and rear segments are of a dark grey satin. The whole larva was delicately hand and machine embroidered for its distinctive markings, body hair and eyes.

28
EMERALD MOTH ON BANKSIA
[1982]

Freestanding sculpture
95 × 35 × 25 (height) cm
Private collection

Although the Emerald Moth (*Praesynocyna semicrocea*) normally camouflages itself under leaves in the daytime, this work shows the setting in which I first discovered one, with its colour tonings so well suited to the lichen on an old banksia log. Camouflage and mimicry are some of the means by which insects successfully survive.

This small green moth, with broad wings and feathery antennae, flies rather slowly and only by night. At rest, it spreads its wings or folds them over its body in a triangle. At night these moths tend to fly towards lights and it is often pitiful to see their damaged wings and antennae.

The twig-like larvae or caterpillars, known as loopers, are foliage feeders and are also well camouflaged on the food plant. The larva pupates in a flimsy silken cocoon, usually among debris on the ground. It looks like a dead twig hanging limply by a strand of larval silk.

Banksia serrata is found in Victoria, Tasmania and New South Wales. It grows to about thirteen metres high in poor coastal sandy soil, with the trunk and branches becoming more gnarled as it ages. The leaves are bright green and brittle, with artificial-looking saw-toothed edges. When I first saw this plant in a florist shop I presumed the florist had cut the leaves with huge pinking shears. On coastal camping trips our children have often played the game of finding the most fearsome-looking banksia nut.

In this textile sculpture the moth's thorax and abdomen were rughooked into canvas using embroidery cottons. The cottons were all left quite long until the whole back was worked. They were then carefully trimmed to shape it into thoracic and abdominal segments.

The moth's wings are of silk organza over green satin, with veins machine stitched. The eyes and proboscis are hand embroidered and the antennae are of trimmed emu feathers. The legs are made of twenty strands of plied machine-sewing threads.

The old banksia log is constructed from silk organza over woollen threads, combed raw wool and silk threads. It is filled with dacron for support. The corrugated and puckered shapes were achieved by hand quilting and sewing. The lichen was made by fraying small squares of crocheted wool, which were then hand sewn to the twigs and log. The serrated banksia leaves are of silk organza, with the seams turned inward, and the details were machine embroidered.

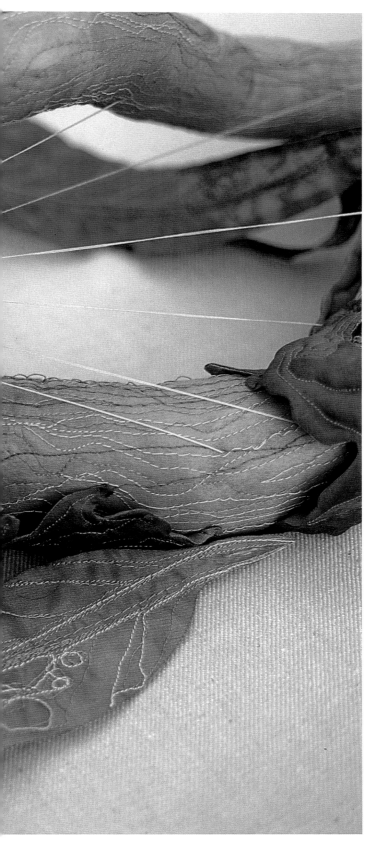

29

FALLEN RED GUM LOG

[1982]

Freestanding sculpture
88 × 42 × 18 (height) cm
Private collection

There are several fine old Red Gums (*Eucalyptus tereticornis*) in the Sale district but unfortunately few young ones. Their numbers have been greatly reduced over the past decades by insect plagues, and by logging for their valuable hardwood. Their trunks and branches have a lot of character as they shed their old bark and reveal the new. In *Fallen Red Gum Log* the smooth, inner, pale new bark is exposed as the rough outer layer of old, darker bark peels off. This contrast of colour and texture is portrayed in the textile branch, with the use of many silk overlays and underlying colour-graded wool. The shape is supported internally with dacron filling and millinery wire. About twenty separate parts were sewn together to form the shape of the log.

Spiders have already inhabited the crevices. Their eggs are tiny, handmade felt balls covered with cream stockings. A delicate silk web clings in the fork of the log. It was crocheted on a wood-and-nail Knitting Nancy frame that my daughter, Joanne, used as a child. The silk gum leaves, in various stages of decomposition, are all separate and are casually tossed over and around the log.

30
FALLEN BRANCHES
[1982]

Flat embroidered wall panel
90 × 90 cm
Sale Regional Arts Centre

*F*allen Branches features a section of the Thom-
son River near the end of Raglan Street in
Sale, just near where we live. When our children
were young it was a favourite family spot for a
splash and paddle and picnic lunch. The old
swinging rope tied to a branch over the water
hangs there still.

I have depicted the low water level of the 1982
drought that revealed the eroded river bank and
exposed the gum roots with the numerous fallen
branches tangled among them. This debris provided a haven for wildlife.

As in *Above the Channels*, the painted surface
was kept unobtrusive and softly blurred by the
use of diluted fabric paint, lightly washed in on a
damp canvas to allow it to bleed slightly, to focus
on the 'framed' area of roots, branches and debris.
The stitched lines of the inner 'frame' follow the
warp and weft of the canvas. This whole detailed
area is very densely embroidered with about
thirty shades and grades of sewing threads varying from dull to glossy and from thick to fine.
Also, different needle sizes (from 60 to 120) and
thread tensions were combined to highlight textures and simulate water, grass, sticks and roots.

Sewing with a thick 120 needle and heavy
buttonhole thread is a tricky procedure with no
room for mistakes as this combination makes
permanent stitch holes in the canvas that would
be unsightly if unpicking were necessary.

The most difficult aspect of this textile was
overcoming the material's tendency to severely
pucker with such intensive sewing, and ensuring
that the work would remain square.

31
SILVEREYES
[1983]

High-relief wall sculpture
100 × 105 × 8 (relief) cm
Sale Regional Arts Centre

This work is designed to radiate the distinctive prissiness and delicacy of the Silvereye (*Zosterops lateralis*), and their sociable and harmonious behaviour. Of all the honeyeaters in my garden Silvereyes are the most attractive and least aggressive. They are present in large flocks and family groups throughout the year, feasting on whatever is in season in the way of nectar, berries and fruit. By far their favourite area in our garden is the stand of Queensland Poplar trees outside our bedroom windows. In the berry season we awake to a choir of Silvereyes singing high-pitched trills.

I found their feather-fall and distinctive feather markings difficult to sketch as they are constantly on the move and it was not until I was given an unfortunate road casualty as a specimen that I was able to complete the work.

Because Silvereyes always stay in dense vegetation, I wanted this wall work to have more density than space. To achieve this I designed the grevillea flowers and leaves (*Grevillea rosmarinifolia* 'Lutea') to lead in around the birds on four levels: a pale paint wash only, a paint wash with surface stitching, heavily detailed stitching, and relief fabric sculpture. This enabled me to prominently feature the Silvereyes, yet still retain the thick foliage and sense of camouflage. Shadows created by the high-relief leaves also add to the three-dimensional effect.

Silvereyes is the most complicated small work I have tackled. It was painstakingly slow to make, as each flower, bud and leaf was embroidered separately. The leaves were made of six different shades of felt from recycled army berets, purchased at the local Aussie Disposals store, that were pinned then stitched together, somewhat like making a jig-saw puzzle.

No. 31, *Silvereyes*, details.

MYTHICAL MOTH SERIES

*T*he series on Mythical Moths evolved from my *Emperor Gum Moth observations. I became acutely aware of the many colour and tonal changes as the moths' wings pumped up and dried out. On close inspection I discovered patches of vivid colour, so I began creating brilliantly coloured moths that were almost like butterflies. This was a new era. In the past I had only worked from real specimens for interpretation and inspiration and all of my works had tended towards the earthy bush tones with only a touch of hard colour. It was a whole new learning process in colour combinations and imaginative design.*

32
AMEINUS McCUBBINONYMOUS, LEPIDOPTERA
[1982]

Freestanding sculpture
30 × 20 × 15 (height) cm
Private collection

This work was designed as a gift for Pat and Charles McCubbin of Longford, Gippsland, in thanks for their encouragement of my art and invaluable advice on natural history. My mythical moth specimen was duly presented – set, pinned and mounted, as is fitting for a collector.

Charles has been a collector of insects all his life and now is a breeder of butterflies. He has a vast knowledge of insects, their life cycles, behaviour and habitats. I am deeply grateful for his generous sharing of his expertise, his dedication and enthusiasm, and have named the work accordingly.

The moth's subtle colour changes were achieved by using a simple direct printing method (sometimes called transfer painting) with fabric paint on silk organza. Different mixtures of coloured paints are strategically poured onto a smooth, flat surface (such as heavy plastic on a tabletop) to form preconceived designs and combinations. Silk is gently pressed on the paint so the colours blend and bleed together on the silk. These silk prints are hung out to dry, then the sections that are best suited to the design are chosen.

Machine embroidery, hand embroidery and appliqué further embellish the wings. Millinery wire supports the wing span.

The specimen is pinned to its mount with an old silver hatpin. This mount also functions as a setting, which is rendered in textile paint diluted to watercolour consistency that repeats the moth's colours, but in different colour proportions. The mauve-pink is accentuated in the sunset area, in which direction the moth is facing. The blue and green of the shrubs and trees repeat these tones in the moth. The whole tiny strip of scene was extensively machine embroidered before being attached to the plastic-sealed cardboard roll that supports it.

Mythical Moth Series

33
MYTHICAL MOTH
[1983]

High-relief wall sculpture
55 × 65 × 6 (relief) cm
Private collection

L ike the previous work, this one is also a
fanciful interpretation of a moth pinned to a
collector's board. The board is represented by the
plain rectangular area on which the moth rests.

The moth's habitat or environment is shown in
the distance, with trees, shrubs, ferns, rocks,
flowers and open grasslands first depicted in fabric
paint. In this case, watercolour painting techniques were used on a backing of dampened linen
to allow the muted paint tones to wash together,
whereas the darker rectangular area was painted
when the linen was dry to provide a sharp, well-
defined contrast. Highlights and fine line details
were machine and hand embroidered to complete
the background setting in a balance and design
that would complement the moth.

During this work I discovered that it was
unnecessary to constantly change the colour of the
bobbin thread to suit the colour of the top thread.
Setting the machine on a slightly tighter bobbin
tension and looser top tension ensured that the
bottom thread colour would not show on the
surface. This seemingly small discovery was a
major time-saver for all future works.

The moth was made in the same way as the one
in *Ameinus McCubbinonymous, Lepidoptera*. It could
also have been a freestanding sculpture, but instead
it has been attached to the backing fabric as a wall
sculpture.

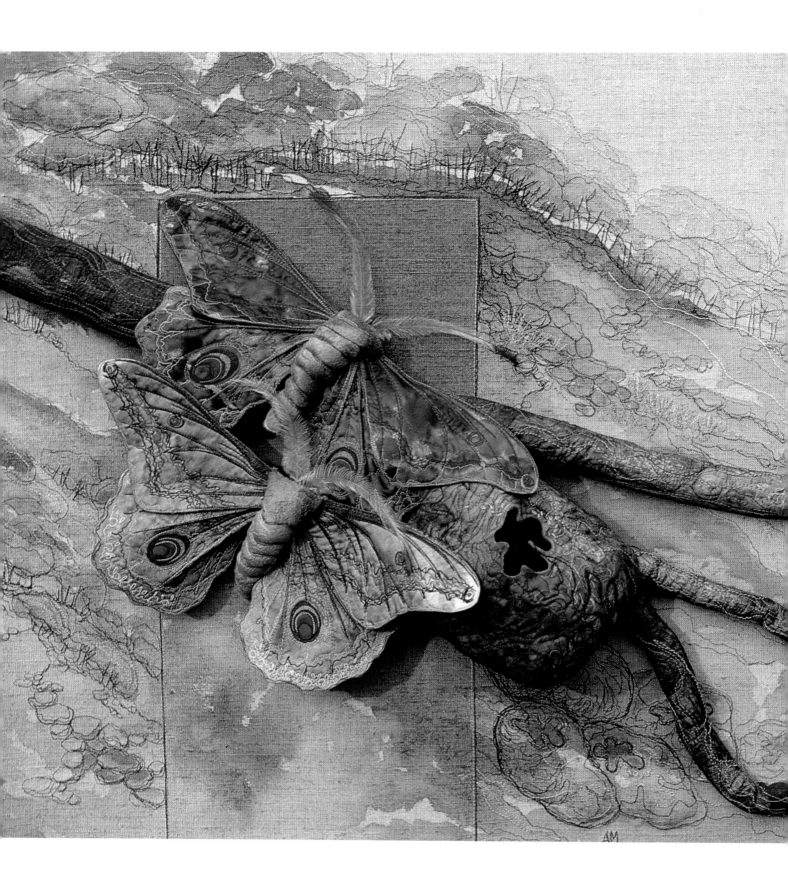

34
MATING MYTHICAL MOTHS
[1984]

High-relief wall sculpture
77 × 117 × 15 (relief) cm
Private collection

This is another in the series of Mythical Moth works that range from freestanding sculptures to flat wall works. *Mating Mythical Moths* is a fanciful interpretation depicting a blue female moth freshly emerged from her cocoon; even before she is ready to fly, she has been sought out by the colourful green male.

The two moths, the cocoon and the branch were actually made in the previous year, but at that stage I was unable to devise adequate support to make the work a totally freestanding sculpture. For me it remains an interim example in the learning process.

The inserted plain rectangle conveys a feeling of space, allows the moths to appear uncluttered and tranquil, and displays them with maximum effectiveness. It also hints that they may be used for the collector's pinning board.

The sewing within the work is mostly machine embroidery, with fine details added by hand. Materials used include fabric paint, silk, linen, synthetic fur fabric, emu feathers, dacron filling, and a variety of embroidery and machine threads.

The more machine sewing there is on a particular area, the more the fabric is pulled in and shrinks, so the more steam-ironing it requires. I have to stop and iron every five or ten minutes to minimise this distortion. The ironing also eliminates unwanted puckering and buckling. It is mostly done on the back but works with large relief areas, like *Mating Mythical Moths*, can only be ironed on the front. I always use a cotton cloth (damp or dry) to protect the stitches from burning or becoming shiny.

35
SLATE PENCIL SEA URCHIN
[1984–87]

Freestanding sculpture
45 × 35 × 25 (height) cm
Private collection

Some of my earliest and happiest memories of living in Australia involve the beach and the sea. Like a bower bird, I loved to collect objects and to examine them closely at home. I would lay them out in rows of colour and kind, and then draw my favourites. I still remember my disappointment when a washed-up sea urchin began to smell. How could anything so beautiful smell so bad?

In this sea urchin (*Phyllacanthus parvispinus*) I have tried to capture the essence of its texture and form. There were many difficulties in pattern drafting and construction. The 'squashed' round shape, an oblate spheroid, was drafted and made in ten separate parts. To prevent it from caving in I had to create a dense structure that would not easily compress or collapse. I used a variation on the trapunto method whereby fibre is threaded between two layers of stitched fabric to raise the level of the top one. On the back of each segment of the urchin I stitched two layers of heavy felt together and stuffed so much dacron between them that the segments became self-supporting and stiff. The ten segments were then carefully joined by hand sewing pairs together to create a five-segmented sea urchin.

Several metres of cream silk organza were painted to simulate the colouration and mottled patterns of the spikes and main form. Small and large painted rectangles of silk were embroidered in detail and stitched into tube shapes to form the spikes. They were packed firmly with dacron wadding so they would remain rigid and stand upright once attached to the urchin. All wools and sewing threads were tied off on the inside of the urchin before it was lined with salmon pink satin. The work was modified in 1987 with more hand embroidery, embellishment and glass beading being added to the rim and spikes to simulate a wet look.

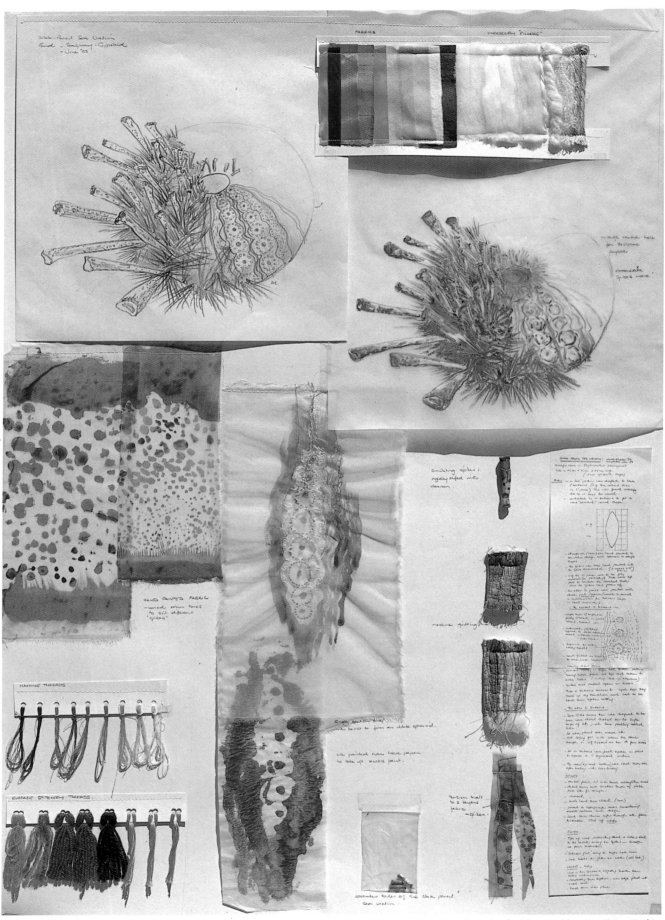

Sampler for No. 35, *Slate Pencil Sea Urchin*.

No. 35, *Slate Pencil Sea Urchin*, details.

36
BARNACLES
[1984–87]

Freestanding sculpture
38 × 38 × 26 (height) cm
Private collection

Some people have interpreted this sculpture as a provocative feminist statement, with suggestive labia, clinging babies and coils of hair. Nothing could have been further from my intentions. Yet it is interesting for me to realise that no shape in nature is entirely novel; so many forms are repeated constantly, others only rarely.

Like the sculptures *Slate Pencil Sea Urchin* and *Mussels and Kelp*, *Barnacles* is influenced by my pleasurable childhood experiences at the beach.

The research and learning process is a very important part of the finished work for me. In my collection I have varieties of barnacles attached to wood, wine bottles, polystyrene, to other shells and to each other. It intrigued me to learn that once the barnacle permanently attaches itself to an object with the cement organs in its atennules, it stands on its head for the rest of its life!

In 1984, while I was driving down the main street in Sale, a truck with a load of huge metal pipes and valves covered with barnacles passed me. I caught up with the truck driver at the traffic lights and asked if I could have a couple of specimens. I could see he thought I was eccentric, but he did pull over and allow me to chisel some barnacles off his pipes. These enormous 8-centimetre-high specimens inspired this sculpture and are still treasured.

The barnacles (*Cirripedia crustacean*) were made by layering cream silk organza over a variety of cream to brown shades of silk, wool, cotton and fabric off-cuts. The central holes were reversed with another layer of silk to prevent fraying and distortion of the designed shape. The large and many small barnacles were intensively machine embroidered employing false-tension sewing, free-sewing, buttonhole cotton to spool, tailor-tacking, and endless plain line-sewing. In false-tension sewing I deliberately alter the normal thread tension settings on the machine by either loosening or tightening the top thread tension, or loosening or tightening the bobbin thread tension. The effects vary according to the fabric and thread used. Here a tight bobbin tension helped pull in and dome the barnacles. Buttonhole cotton to spool is the technique of winding very heavy thread that will not go through the eye of a machine needle around the bobbin by hand, turning the work upside down and sewing blind so that the thread appears on the surface of the work. I used this for the thick, wiry seaweed-like growths on the barnacles. I used the machine's tailor-tacking foot and fine cream silk thread for the wide, dense zig-zag stitches that curl and bunch like filaments. Quilting, hand sewing, padding, sculpting and stuffing were also used – and a great deal of improvisation – to achieve the effect of layer on layer of barnacles.

Many reels of unravelled sewing cotton threads were twined and tied in place to simulate the surrounding swirling seaweed.

As with the *Slate Pencil Sea Urchin*, in later years I felt this sculpture needed more 'oomph' and a 'wet from the sea' look. Thus many cream, glass and pearl beads were hand sewn over the surface to catch the light and glisten like water droplets.

In 1988 this work toured with the Ararat Gallery's 4th Biennial Exhibition of Fibre and Textiles.

37
MUSSELS AND KELP
[1983]

Freestanding sculpture
109 × 36 × 20 (height) cm
Sale Regional Arts Centre

*M*ussels and Kelp was inspired by a camping holiday at the junction of the sea and the Mueller River in Gippsland. After a night of severe storms, mounds of kelp were washed up on the shore, and all sorts of sea treasures were trapped among them.

This work gives totally different impressions depending on the angle from which it is viewed. For example, from the back, only the tough outer shells are visible. Their colour tones are muted, but there is a hint of movement in the hairy threads. When viewed from the front, the whole cluster of mussels springs to life. The shells are open, exposing the brilliant contrasting colours and textures of the inner flesh.

Extensive use of textural variations has helped create the surface image of the shells and seaweed. Numerous shades of shimmering silk and satin create the 'almost wet' look of the mussels' inner flesh. These parts have been minimally stitched to retain as much shine (and smoothness of texture) on the fabric as possible. The outer shells are of silk organza, hand painted and then layered over variously coloured wools so the graded shades show through the silk. These layers are intensively machine stitched to represent the roughened shell, growth layers and grooves. Brown sewing threads hang free from the back of the shells to create a sense of movement and flow in the sculpture.

The kelp is entirely of felt. Natural brown, grey and cream fleece was bound inside pantyhose stockings to obtain the required shapes, and then felted. This was possible thanks to the expertise of Mrs Anna Camin of Sale. I then dyed the felt in shades of brown and decoratively stitched it to obtain a kelp-like texture.

Mussels and Kelp was selected for the Bicentennial national touring exhibition, 'The Face of Australia', in 1988.

38
WATTLE SEED-PODS
[1984]

Freestanding tactile sculpture
Six pods each approximately 45 × 8 × 5 (height) cm,
seed cluster 26 × 13 × 4 (height) cm
Private collection

Wattle Seed-pods illustrates my interest in progressive botanical changes.

A tall and stately Cootamundra Wattle (*Acacia baileyana*) in our garden provided the inspiration for this work. This silver-hued tree is attractive most of the year, whether covered in masses of yellow balls, seed-pods or new purple leaf tips.

The textile sculpture shows the colour and textural variations that occur during the maturation process of the Cootamundra Wattle seed-pods. The pods range from greens and browns to purple. The last seed-pod is gnarled and split, exposing the new seeds.

The second part of the sculpture shows the seeds fallen to the ground and resting on leaves and twigs. The cycle is ready to start again.

This sculpture was also made to be handled, and as it is in seven separate parts it can be moved and rearranged at will. I find it interesting to see how others like it arranged.

The subtle colour gradations and changes were created by bleeding textile paint into two layers of fine silk organza. A lot of fabric is wasted as not all the dyed fabric is suitable, but the technique is very rewarding because the painterly effects are unique.

Free-sewing (with tight bobbin tension) around the edges of the pods warped and puckered the silk and therefore accentuated the central smooth swellings where the seeds lay. More sewing produces more warping, so only a little was added to the lush green pod in contrast to the gnarled open one. This is the only work I have never ironed because the puckered and distorted surface is just what I wanted here. Normally, ironing is a constant and monotonous chore throughout the making of my textile works.

Other than a great deal of hand embroidery, techniques such as quilting, stuffing, wiring and moulding were used to obtain the desired effects. The seeds exposed by the split pod were moulded from soft leather over rounded beach pebbles.

The delicate wattle leaves were made by stitching then trimming felt into finely divided fronds with surgical scissors.

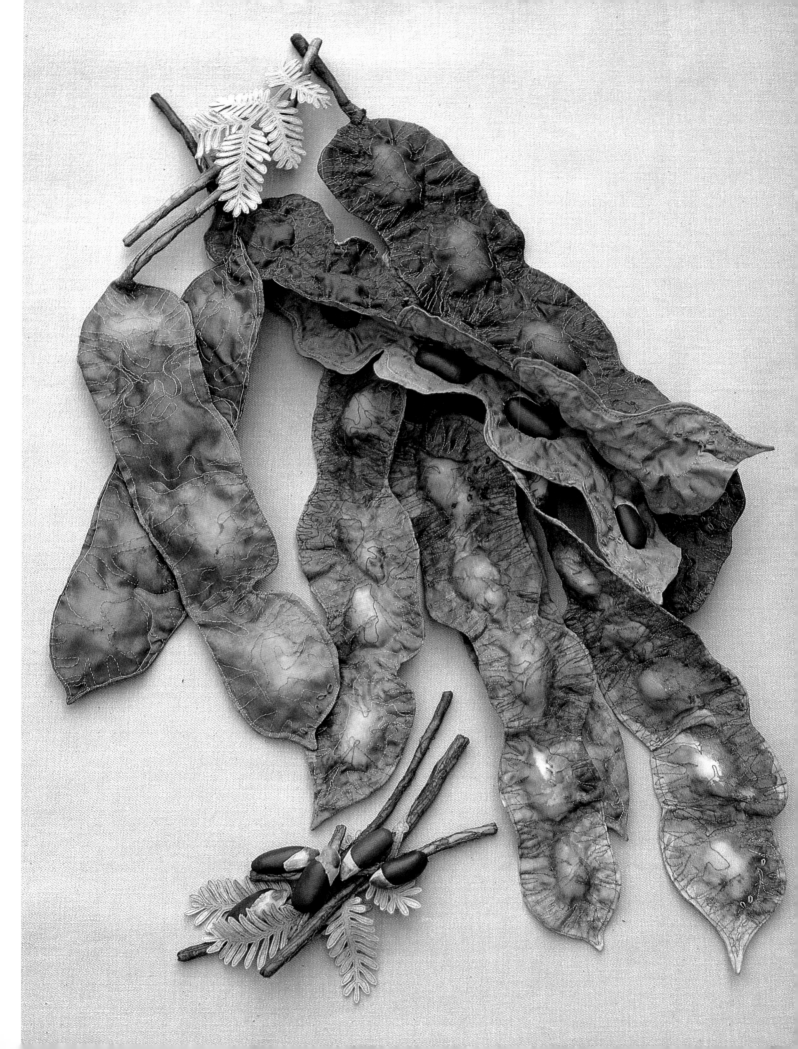

39
HERE SHE COMES!
[1983]

Low-relief wall panel
45 × 85 cm
Private collection

*H*ere She Comes! is a very personal work and is included in this book because it was so popular with the public when exhibited. It seems I am not the only one who sees people in birds and vice versa. It was specifically designed for my mother-in-law Alma Mein's 72nd birthday. The eleven chicks represent her eleven grandchildren – Geoff, Sandy, Jackie, Bruno, Peter, Ian, Rosemary, Kate, Alysia, Joanne and Fiona. I have written a family story about this work and each grandchild knows his or her position on the perch.

Alma's love for, and selfless sharing with, her grandchildren, and the fact that she is an excellent cook (partly due to her former profession as a home economics teacher), ensure that they not only adore her but also her cooking. *Here She*

Comes! is a statement of love for Alma and the family that stems from her. In a sense, it is a family portrait.

The birds are loosely based on the Yellow Robin but this is by no means a normal Yellow Robin family. Even when robins only have two or three chicks to feed it must seem like a case of never-ending, bottomless pits. The exaggerated number of fledglings represent the feelings of the parent – any parent, feathered or not – at meal preparation time.

Fabric paint (mixed to a watercolour wash consistency) and delicate linear stitching convey the impression of mist and fog still hanging on the ridges and in the gully. At first light the parent bird bravely starts the early feeding-round. The chicks are huddled together for warmth, company and security, with the ones on the outer edges looking somewhat discomfited and chilly. Maybe these outer ones are irritated by the noisy chirpings, or still sleepy, or perhaps they are the ones that were fed last time. The wide open spaces have been deliberately designed to focus on and accentuate the chicks. The pale khaki canvas backing also adds to the visual impact of the gaping, insistent yellow beaks.

Here She Comes!, detail.

No. 39, *Here She Comes!*

40
EARLY BIRDS
[1985]

Low-relief wall panel
63 × 51 cm
City of Box Hill

This small work was made purely for pleasure and relaxation during my two-year commitment to the six historical bas-relief bronze sculptures for Sale's pedestrian mall. Prior to this bronze commission I had intended to do a series of works on a variety of juvenile birds. I was interested in the subtleties of expression in eyes, beaks and stance and I had done countless sketches in preparation for this. The concept of a bird series stemmed from the response to the work *Here She Comes!* but only two of the works have been completed so far.

In *Early Birds* the two birds represent some of the earliest risers in the Gippsland bush – juvenile Superb Blue Wrens (*Malurus cyaneus*). The interpretation of their expressions is left to the viewer. Are they cold or hungry or does one see mother approaching? In the background, sunlight is just beginning to seep through the trees into the valley, heralding the dawn.

41
LEPIDOPTERA QUADRIPARTITE
[1985]

High-relief wall sculpture with wearable art
152 × 32 × 10 (relief) cm
Private collection

This four-part work was specifically made to have the dual function of 'wearable art' and a wall sculpture. The highly decorative green silk moth and the long trail of gum leaves unclip from the panel to form a necklace and headpiece to match the khaki-coloured dress. Their velcro attachment is concealed underneath the panel's sculpted cocoons. The moth had to be perfectly weight-balanced to hang straight and even at the wing tips. This was my first use of glass beads. I liked the added texture and light-capturing effects for decorative textiles and have used beading many times since.

This particular work poignantly reminded me of my childhood in Haarlem, Holland. Its shape, stitching and silken texture were similar to my maternal grandparents' cigar-box embroideries. I still remember the joys of handling and playing with these *lapjes* (meaning patches or rags) and how my patient grandfather allowed me to cover his reclining body with them. When working today, I reflect on the strange workings of fate.

Lepidoptera Quadripartite was designed for the Gippsland Craft Council 'Wearable Craft Exhibition and Parade', celebrating Victoria's 150th birthday in 1985.

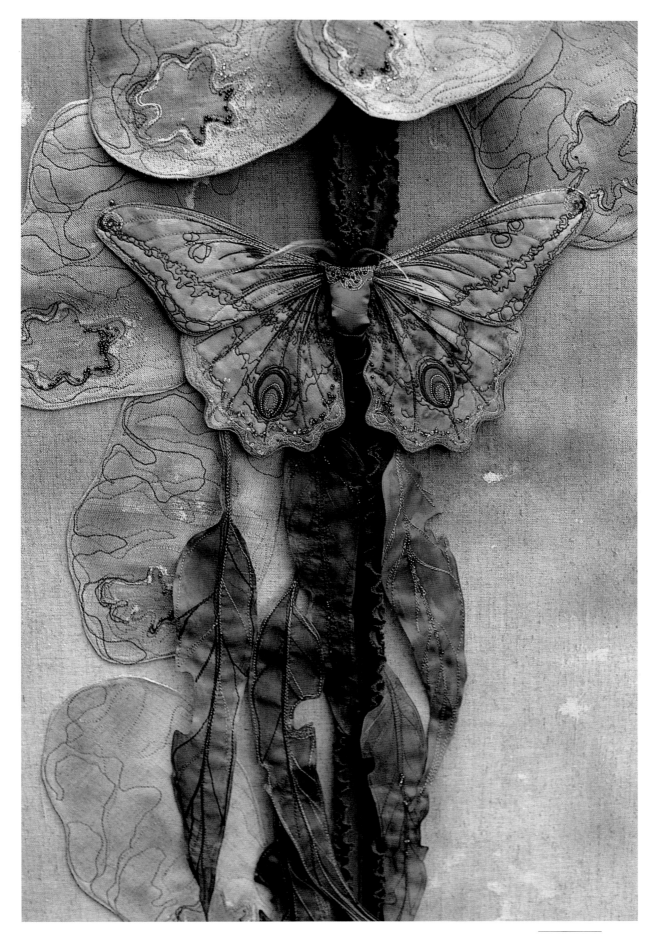

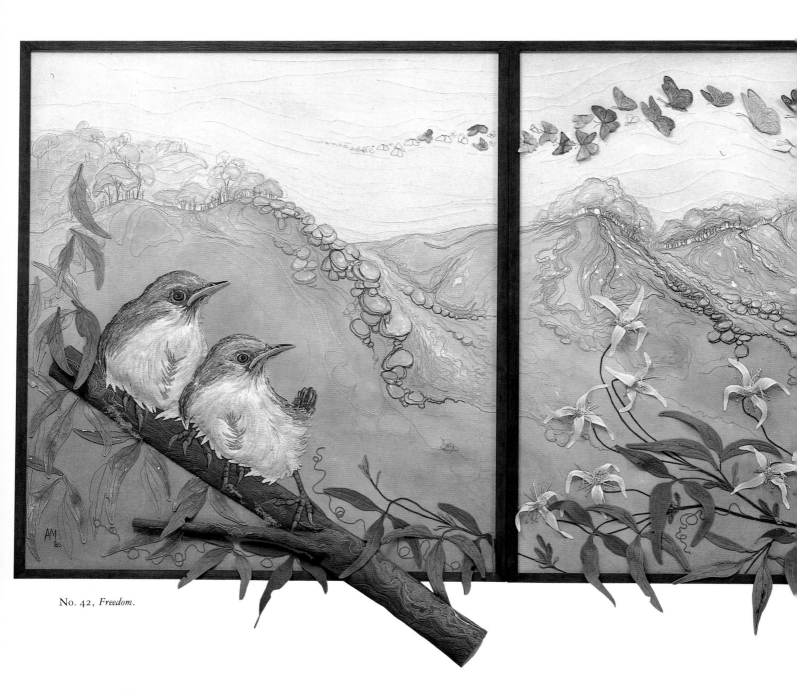

No. 42, *Freedom*.

42
FREEDOM
[1986]

*High-relief wall sculpture in three panels with
relief sections extending beyond the frame
and detachable moth
140 × 100 × 10 (relief) cm each panel
Private collection*

On 10 December 1985 I made a site inspection for this commission, and on the same
day I attended the opening of the Butterfly House
at the Royal Melbourne Zoo. These excursions,
together with my previous experience with Charles
McCubbin of releasing butterflies within the
butterfly enclosure, inspired the design concept.
Releasing the butterflies into that superb spacious
setting was a very moving experience. I have tried
to portray that in the work. The commissioner's
entrance foyer, with its cathedral ceilings and
vast areas of glass merging the garden outside
with the interior, was ideally suited to a flight of
butterflies.

Freedom has more colour, paint and relief areas
than I had used together in one work before. To
me, this work is a kaleidoscope of merging colour
combinations. Developing the colour composition was very time-consuming as I wanted to
ensure the correct interactions of dominance,
blending, grading and optical illusion.

SCENE The painted and stitched mountain
range portrayed in *Freedom* is a view from our bush
block in Briagolong. A lot of my artistic stimulus
comes from this delightful area along the Blackall
Creek. In the summer of 1985 the Common
Brown Butterfly was there in plague proportions,
providing me with excellent opportunities to
draw and to study the movement of butterflies
in flight.

The three panels were designed to fit precisely
together. I used the mountain range and butterfly
flight to break up the edges of the frame and lead
the eye around the composition.

BUTTERFLIES About forty butterflies (and
two moths) covering twenty-five different Australian species have been depicted in varying
degrees of detail. I used artistic licence to tone up
or tone down the butterflies' colours to specifically suit the overall design and flow of the flight:
a hot orange butterfly might become a shade of
tan, for example. I wanted the butterflies to
complement each other rather than to highlight
individuals. In the research stage I found that the

reproduction of butterfly colours varied greatly between reference books. Where possible, I used my own collected specimens as references. The embroidered butterflies are not anatomically perfect but they are distinctly recognisable species.

Achieving a 'natural' grading of size, colour and flow through the flight of butterflies was probably the most difficult part of the whole work.

All the butterflies were painted on silk organza, then machine and hand embroidered for distinctive details and wing patterns. Their placement in semi-relief on the backing canvas adds to the credibility of their angles and foreshortened wings.

BIRDS Two juvenile Tailorbirds (*Cisticola exilis*) are huddled together watching the butterflies with awe and apprehension. The one closest to the butterflies is pushing his sibling, who is struggling to balance. They were made in several pieces and when the eyes, beaks and feather details were stitched, the parts were all stuffed with dacron and quilted into semi-relief on the canvas. The outline of their breast bones is just visible to give a young and not-quite-feathered look. Both beaks are angled to mirror the butterfly flight, and to direct the eye back to the butterflies.

LOG The birds' perch was made in the round like a freestanding sculpture. The colour-graded silk surface was stitched and embellished to simulate wood-grain, with the aid of variations in stitch tension.

COCOONS The cocoons were painted on pieces of canvas then stitched, padded, reverse-seamed and quilted into place. There was much juggling and rearranging so that they were in balance with both the angle of the butterfly flight and the birds' log.

FLOWERS Specimens of Australian clematis (*Clematis aristata*) were collected at Golden Beach near Sale. They had a delicate, unobtrusive quality that suited the central panel. The petals and leaves were made to sit in semi-relief, with plied cotton and French knots used for their stamens. Several leaves hang free over the frame to break up the dominant bottom frame-line.

BOGONG MOTH The relief Bogong Moth (*Agrotis infusa*) sits on two cocoons and is able to be removed as it is attached with a velcro fastener. It was designed to enhance the arch of the butterfly flight from right to left, while the birds' perch points to it, leading the eye from the perch back to the Bogong Moth.

43
FREEDOM SAMPLERS
[1986]

Seven low-relief wall panels
Paint-wash trial II
68 × 58 cm
Tailorbird sampler
60 × 50 cm
Completed Tailorbird
50 × 40 cm
Clematis sampler
63 × 55 cm
Cocoon sampler
63 × 62 cm
Pink heath sampler
63 × 55 cm
Butterfly construction sampler
58 × 60 cm
Sale Regional Arts Centre

ABOVE Tailorbird sampler.
BELOW Completed Tailorbird.

These seven small works are the trials and errors, leftovers and experimental sewing samplers from the main work *Freedom*. They have been mounted and collaged together to show the stages of construction and the stitch techniques, threads and fabrics used. All labels and wording in the samplers were written in machine-stitched freehand.

Freedom went on exhibition at the Sale Regional Arts Centre prior to installation in the commissioner's home. Sketches, draft design layouts and a final pencil-on-paper design, and these seven samplers were also displayed. This 'total' exhibition was equally popular with art students and the general public and gave them a clearer understanding of the many processes involved in creating one major work. The Sale Regional Arts Centre purchased the drawings and samplers as teaching aids.

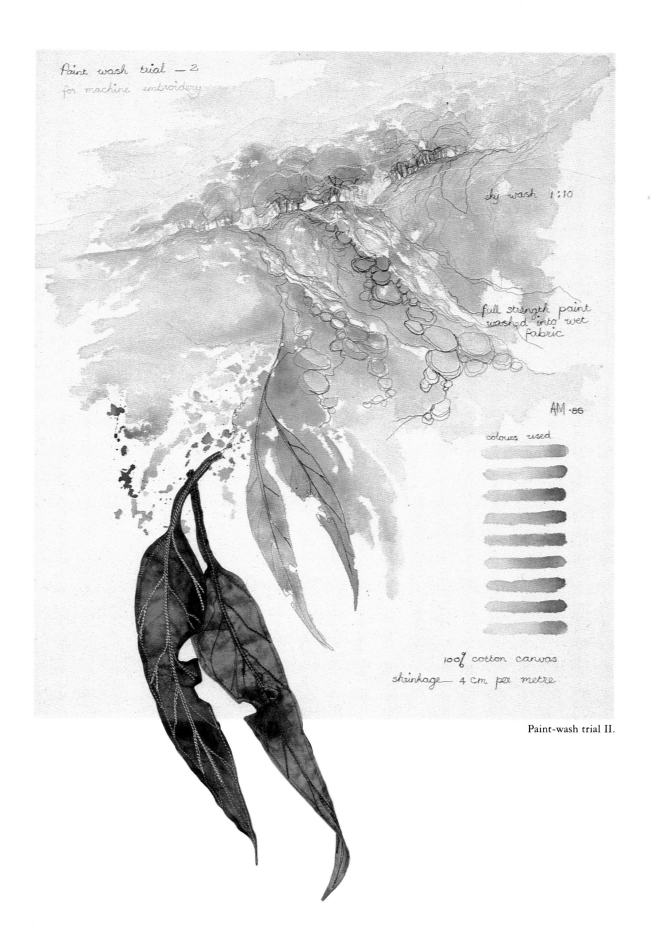

Paint wash trial — 2
for machine embroidery

sky wash 1:10

full strength paint
washed into wet
fabric

AM ·86

colours used

100% cotton canvas
shrinkage — 4 cm per metre

Paint-wash trial II.

No. 43, Clematis sampler.

point colours

lining — quilting

machine threads

AM80

Pot Sampler

free sewing

No. 43, Cocoon sampler.

canvas and paints used
machine threads
appliqué – cotton and spun wool – grass
carpet wool – flowers
free sewing method over carpet wool
Pink Heath Sampler
AM
No. 43, Pink heath sampler.

No. 43, Butterfly construction sampler.

44
NIGHT FLIGHT
[1986]

High-relief wall sculpture with detachable moths
91 × 111 × 7 (relief) cm
Private collection

One of the delightful things about living in the country town of Sale is the local public support and interest shown in my work. People from all walks of life have helped my creativity and development, not only as an artist but also as a human being. Many have given me their old felt hats, pre-war silk stockings, furs, army trousers and silk frocks.

Night Flight stemmed from this generosity. I was given the off-cut scraps of heavy woven upholstery cotton from the refurbishing of a friend's lounge suite. My love of fabrics will be apparent throughout this book. These pieces were so tactile and had a richness of pattern and colour like a Persian carpet, that the image of moths and cocoons immediately came to my mind. Before I realised it, I was sketching out a design.

The upholstery fabric was a dense weave with about twenty-one colours incorporated in its warp and weft. It also tended to change colour in different light, making it extremely difficult to consistently match with other fabric. To suit this complex weave of colours, I dyed eighteen different shades of fabric to make the insect wings harmonise.

The upholstery fabric cocoons are all regular in size and shape, and are woven together like honeycomb. To prevent monotony, I removed some sections altogether, and line-stitched or painted in the repeating shapes. The hill in the scene also mirrors the cocoon shapes and leads down to them.

The moths are all facing inwards and upwards towards the moon in a typical movement to the light. Once again the metamorphic change from ugly grub to beautiful insect is depicted. Five of the moths are removable and can be worn if desired.

The whole work is a collage of paint, lustre, beads, fur, fur fabric, metallic thread, fishing line, net, dacron, satin, velvet, silk, rayon, canvas, pipe cleaners, and in fact almost anything that matched the original upholstery fabric.

There was a nice twist when I invited my friend to see what I had made with her fabric. She bought the work on the spot, and it hangs above the same couch from which the original off-cuts came.

45
FANTAIL RHAPSODY
[1987]

High-relief wall sculpture with relief sections
extending beyond the frame
165 × 170 × 12 (relief) cm
Private collection

Inspiration for the design of *Fantail Rhapsody* was stimulated by my first daylight visit to the commissioners' house on Lake Glenmaggie in August 1986. The house itself and its spectacular setting with panoramic views of water, hills and bush affected all my senses with their beauty, space, serenity and welcoming charm. Only the bird-songs broke the silence. I have tried to capture these initial impressions in the work.

When choosing the colours, I aimed at complementing the existing interior decor in the open-plan foyer/lounge/dining-room areas. In the design I wanted to arrest the senses with an overwhelming and detailed vision of some of the common flora and fauna in the area.

I also tried to capture the sense of bird noise, particularly through the interaction of four siblings all demanding food at once. The parent bird (*Rhipidura fuliginosa*) is portrayed gently and patiently doing the best it can under the circumstances. Both male and female fantails are identical in feather markings and colouration, so it is up to the viewer to decide the sex of the parent bird.

I chose four fledgling fantails because the commissioners have four (now adult) offspring, and it tickled my fancy that the work might remind them of their labours when their family was young.

The title *Fantail Rhapsody* was chosen to suggest both the noise that young birds make while feeding, and the commissioners' love of music. A rhapsody has been defined as 'an emotional musical composition of indefinite form', which seemed quite appropriate for the young fantails.

Some statistics of interest relevant to this work are: I used an average of six sewing-machine bobbins of thread daily, and over a hundred reels of thread altogether. I worked 1053 hours – not including 'mulling it over' time – and the work took exactly seven months from site inspection to framed completion.

SCENE The distant Grey Box (*Eucalyptus microcarpa* hybrid) and view of Lake Glenmaggie are as accurate as I could execute with needle and thread. This is the view as seen from the lounge, though in reality it is much closer than it is in my

portrayal. The vast expanse of water and trees seems to bring the outdoors inside, and I often felt I was sitting up in a tree and could just reach down and touch the lake.

I also veered from reality to suit the design by eliminating all other trees on the lake's edge. The use of the single big Grey Box avoids cluttering the design. Also this tree is the focal point of the action because a section of it has been superimposed on the foreground and that is where the birds are being fed.

Over thirty different machine-thread colours were used on the scene alone, ranging from silk and cotton to polyester, all varying in thickness and tension. Like the actual scene, my textile work changes colour and mood according to the light.

Due to the size of the canvas, a temporary extension of my sewing bench was essential. Although the main sewing areas on the canvas were deliberately designed to be on the right side, a great deal of 'attachment' sewing had to be done on the left side as well. The whole work would not fit rolled up under the arm of the sewing machine, so all parts on the left were stitched upside-down.

FANTAILS

Fantails were chosen because of their abundance at Lake Glenmaggie, as well as their colour suitability for the commissioners' wall. Once again I used a great deal of artistic licence in the colours. For instance, the blue-mauve tinges to the chicks' head and wing feathers represent that distinctive sheen given off by the quills of not-fully-developed feathers. The beak interiors are more orange-yellow in reality but a soft salmon pink suited the home's interior far better. And the adult bird has more dull brown colouration in its back feathers but I preferred to bring out the grey as seen in soft natural light.

The stitched action lines around the tail of the adult and the wings and toes of the chicks bring the whole work together in a feeling of movement, capturing a particular moment.

A great deal of stitching had to be done by hand so as not to distort the thickness and angles. I simulated machine stitches so these parts would be in keeping with the rest of the birds' stitching and feathery texture. The execution of their beaks, eyes, 'whiskers', feathery breasts and scaly legs was very exacting to achieve that distinct avian look and liveliness of posture and expression.

GREY BOX LEAVES

The leaf specimens were collected from the tree depicted in the scene. The leaves' colours changed dramatically under various light and climatic conditions. Sometimes they were a silver-green, then a dark blue-green varying to a hard green. The new shoots ranged through many shades from apple green to dark purple. The leaves also varied in size and shape. Some were quite oval, even heart-shaped, while others were pointed. Some were wavy and curly and others smooth and flat. What they all did have in common was abundant gall growths from wasp infestation, and many eaten-out holes and chunks where insects had previously dined.

Mature Leaves Nineteen large leaves were made from three different shades of gabardine. I had difficulty finding matching shades but eventually purchased the two paler ones at Job's Warehouse in Melbourne. The darker gabardine was my husband's old English-made raincoat. He graciously surrendered it to me for the sake of art! I found this older fabric far superior in quality to the new. Each leaf has been reversed with matching fabric so that no seams show.

The fabric was cut on the cross to allow stress-steam moulding, stretching and shape-sculpting later, as all the leaves were to be in semi-relief. Woven fabric can only be successfully manipulated when it is cut diagonally to the warp and weft. Then, with the aid of steam and strong pressure, it can be made to bend, curl or twist as desired. The leaves were also partially hand dyed in a darker green to increase the illusion of light and shade and three dimensions according to their placement in the total design. Finally, they were machine stitched, then hand embroidered with vein lines, marks and blemishes in many different shades of cotton and silk. Seven of the leaves were designed to hang outside the frame. I had not used this effect so extensively before and was very pleased with the way the leaves broke the lines of the frame, linking the textile and the mounting wall together.

New Shoots I chose to incorporate a number of clusters of new shoots as their colours particularly suited the colour scheme and overall design. They were made from two layers of silk organza, hand painted and machine embroidered for vein details. They have only been attached to the backing canvas at the stems and through some veins so as to be in semi-relief.

The colours of the clustered new shoots were carefully planned to keep the deep pink, mauve and purple tones near the birds' pink open beaks, and generally away from the cream embroidered blossoms.

GALLS

Fresh specimens of these galls looked a textural delight, clustered onto the surface of the leaves. They ranged in colours from deep magenta, mauves, pale pink to hot pink, and all shades of green that toned in with the leaves. The galls added such a tactile and visual quality to the leaves, and they suited my planned colour scheme so well, that I decided to execute them in high relief rather than just having stitched suggestions of them.

Each individual gall was handmade from silk organza, some of which I dyed specifically. They have been padded out with various shades of wool underneath to allow the padding colours to glow through the silk. They have been hand stitched to each other in bundled groups, and then hand stitched to the leaves to suit the design.

GUM BLOSSOMS The many stages of gum blossom development are depicted in the work. The open blooms are made of hand and machine embroidery, and thousands of French knots.

Some of the gum buds have been painted directly onto the backing canvas and then just machine embroidered to appear further away, but most have been made to sit in high relief. This process required a great deal of time and patience. Small tubes of varying shades of green to blue silk organza were stitched on the machine, turned inside out and stuffed with various shades of wool. This allowed the stuffing colours to show through slightly and gave the visual appearance of light and shadow and colour variation to the buds. The stalk ends of the tubes were quilted in to form the bud shape, and finally machined to the backing canvas. Their placement was critical to have them appear natural and alive.

GUM NUTS The gum nuts were simply outlined in stitches to balance the dead branch and avoid cluttering the work with dominant dark brown colouring.

STEMS AND BRANCHES Three different methods were used to make the branches. First, the main branches were made separately from the backing canvas. About six tones of wool were overlaid with pale green silk organza. This strip was then heavily embroidered in tones of thread to create a woody look on the silk's surface. It was machined into place with gum buds and new leaf shoots camouflaging the joins. Accuracy in pattern drafting was critical to get just the right size, shape and angle for the branches, let alone have them join precisely where designed. Secondly, smaller twigs and branches leading to the flower clusters were painted then machined. And finally, the dead branch of spun wool was included to help blend scene and foreground together.

WORM Fantails normally catch their food 'on the wing' – airborne insects. The fantail family living in my urban garden in Sale have become quite tame and are also accustomed to pieces of cheese or sausage flying their way. I have only seen them get a worm once, and that tiny worm was right where a piece of cheese landed. However, the worm's colour and shape suited my design so I used artistic licence as I doubt whether fantails would normally gather worms in the wild. The worm is at the viewer's eye level so the colour of the morsel to be fed to the demanding chick was vital. Over the months I pinned up to fifty different shades of fabric to the design for assessment of the effect. Finally I decided on salmon pink satin, covered by fine dark brown silk organza. Just enough of the satin shines through the silk without overpowering the work. The worm was made as a long thin tube, embroidered, bent and pulled into shape and finally attached to the beak and canvas backing. I wanted its angle and length to be in exact alignment with the feeding chick's beak, and all the other chicks' eyes had to focus on it as well.

No. 45, *Fantail Rhapsody*, details.

SMALL WORKS

Most of my textiles are large by embroidery stan-dards. I prefer to make my subjects larger than life and be able to play up a specific aspect of interest: for example, the texture of the feather-fall on a bird, or the tonal variations on an insect's wing. In a large work this can be done in dramatically bold stitching and fabric appliqué.

Several of my small works started off as experiments. or technique samplers for larger works. Often I get so carried away with the small design that it is completed as a work in its own right, but invariably I wish I had started on larger backing fabric. That is a common experience for me with large works also, and sometimes I join canvases together to create more fabric space.

The only time I actually completed a small work and a large work with the same subject was for Lewin Honeyeater Nestlings I *and* II, *and even then the two works were different since the composition emphasis changed with the size of the work.*

Small Works
46
FANTAIL NIGHT WATCH
[1987]

Low-relief wall panel
80 × 60 cm
Private collection

Fantail Night Watch was designed from the many sketches drawn for *Fantail Rhapsody*.

By having the bird (*Rhipidura fuliginosa*), the nest and the twig 'hanging in space', I have tried to convey the solitude of the parent's lengthy confinement while incubating eggs. It also helps create a hesitant and somewhat anxious atmos-phere around the bird. As well, the bird's eye has the optical illusion of following the viewer around the room.

The half-moon, the moonlit valley and the yellow painted glow all create an aura of mystery.

47
SOUTHERN BLUE GUM BLOSSOMS
[1987]

Low-relief wall panel
90 × 60 cm
Private collection

Over the past twenty years I have drawn, painted and embroidered gum blossoms in many different techniques. None are as pleasing to me as this example of Southern Blue Gum blossoms (*Eucalyptus globulus*) using French knots. The knots are of different thread thicknesses ranging from fine single-strand silk to six-strand embroidery cotton. I have found that the raised texture effect that is unique to French knots, together with thread thickness and colour variation, are ideal to portray the characteristic fluffiness of gum blossoms.

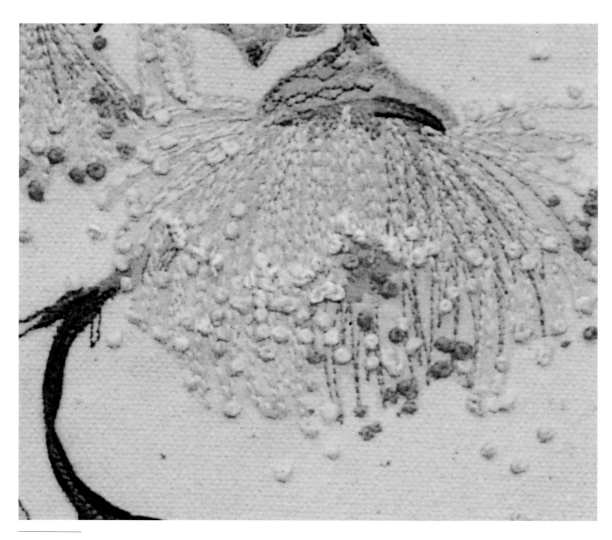

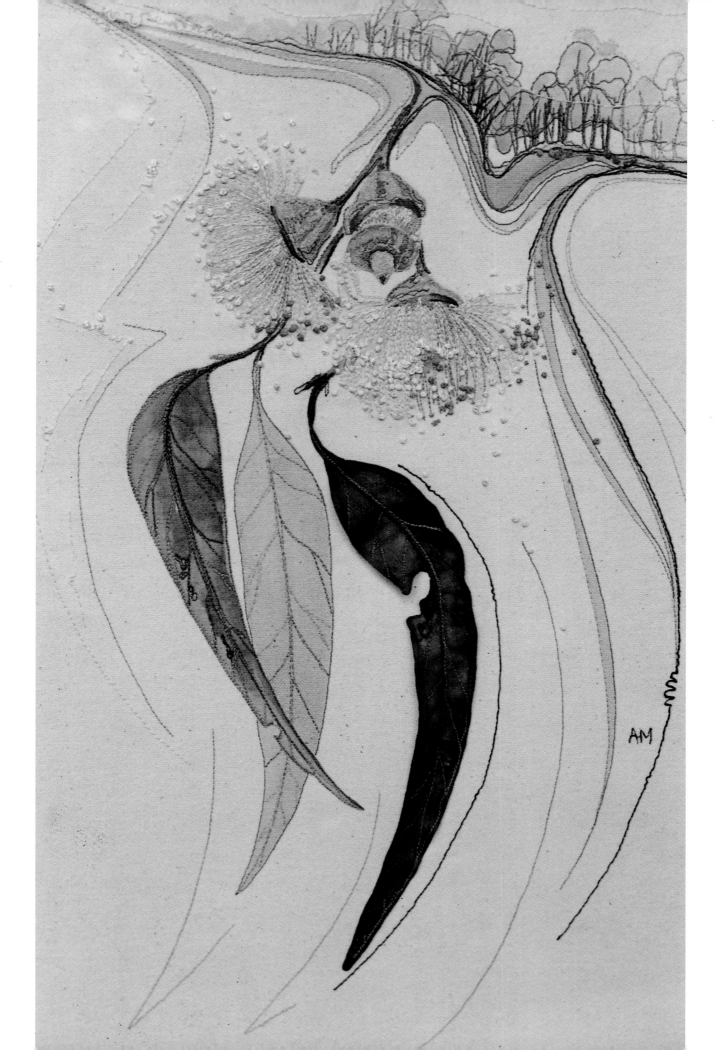

48
FLIGHT DUST
[1987]

Low-relief wall panel
60 × 40 cm
Private collection

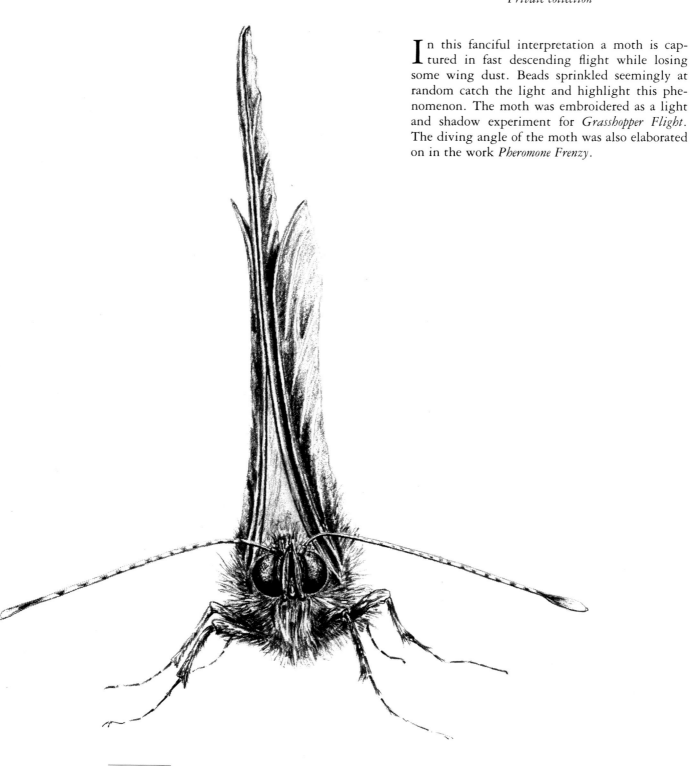

In this fanciful interpretation a moth is captured in fast descending flight while losing some wing dust. Beads sprinkled seemingly at random catch the light and highlight this phenomenon. The moth was embroidered as a light and shadow experiment for *Grasshopper Flight*. The diving angle of the moth was also elaborated on in the work *Pheromone Frenzy*.

49
BUTTERFLY DUST
[1988]

Low-relief wall panel
73 × 55 cm
Private collection

This imaginative butterfly was made for the photographer of many of my works in this book, Walter Sholl, and his wife, Pam.

Each wing is entirely constructed from uncombed, dyed, raw wool layered underneath very fine black silk fabric. This resembles the methods used in making wool pictures. In previous works wool was used sparingly and only in small areas. Surface machine and hand embroidery follows the patterns created by the wool colours and contours. Minute ends of wool protrude through the fine silk, giving the butterfly a natural tactile quality and simulating the texture of real butterfly wings remarkably closely.

AM

Small Works

50
PITTOSPORUM
SEED-PODS
[1987]

Flat embroidered wall panel
20 × 25 cm
Private collection

ABOVE *Pittosporum* seed-pods, deep-etched from backing fabric.
OPPOSITE *Pittosporum* blossoms, deep-etched from backing fabric.

Small Works

5 1
PITTOSPORUM BLOSSOMS
[1987]

Flat embroidered wall panel
20 × 25 cm
Private collection

*P*ittosporum Seed-pods and *Pittosporum Blossoms* are specimen studies of one of my favourite garden trees, *Pittosporum undulatum*. We have a line of them that arches over our driveway and is a haven for native birds.

Both of these small works were painted on silk organza, then the delicate details were embroidered on the machine. It is quite a tricky process as such fine silk tends to damage, wrinkle or pucker very easily. I used the free-sewing technique, supporting the fabric's tension with my hands rather than using a rigid embroidery hoop.

The raised orange seed clusters were made with two layers of zig-zag satin stitch. Bands of heavy satin stitches juxtaposed at different angles catch the light in varying intensities, which increases their three-dimensional qualities.

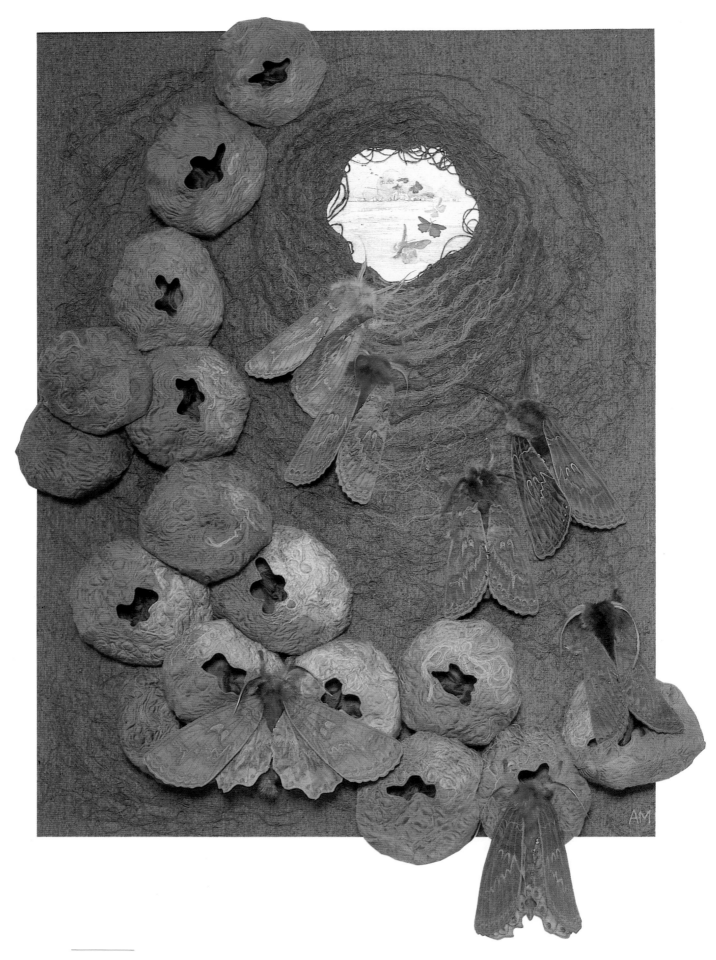

52
FABRIC FANTASY
[1987]

High-relief wall sculpture with relief sections
extending beyond the frame
153 × 105 × 10 (relief) cm
Benalla Art Gallery

This work is an expression of the fascination, awe and wonder I feel when contemplating the metamorphic stages of all insects. I have concentrated on capturing my feelings by depicting aspects of metamorphosis and conveying their mysteries, the insects' instinct for survival and sense of purpose, and their sometimes hidden beauty.

The moths are loosely based on the shape of the Bogong Moth, and the cocoons on those of the Emperor Gum Moth. The dark underground setting is typical of most insects' metamorphic stage, which occurs in 'hidden places' such as underground, under leaves, in cracks or crevices.

Fabric Fantasy shows seven moths in various stages of hatching or drying off before flight. The culmination of their life cycle is imminent. Many moths have already flown away. It is late afternoon, and the sun's rays are low and they glitter on the horizon.

Thirteen cocoons are open, while three are still to hatch. The cocoons and moths are in high relief to give added tactile and visual impressions to their textured and sculptured surfaces.

Moths and other insects can appear to be different colours in different light. Here I have designed them to have warmer colour tones towards the sunlit hole, ranging to cooler colours down into the depths of the crevice.

The background fabric is woven with a wool and synthetic blend. The warp and weft, with their different colouration and texture, have been unravelled from spare fabric and reapplied to the surface in a tunnel shape. Some darker brown hand-spun wool has been added to create more depth, together with some paler yellow and tan commercial wool to give highlights near the hole's entrance.

The moths' wings are made of hand-painted satin and silk organza, their bodies are of fur and felt, and the antennae are of emu and chicken feathers, which are easily replaceable when damaged. All parts have been extensively machine and hand embroidered, with beads added for highlights.

The cocoons are of two layers of silk organza in various tones, with combed wool, spun wool, dyed silk scraps, machine threads and commercial wool between the two layers. They were then stitched together with a tight bobbin tension on the machine to achieve a quilted look. They were hand sculpted into domes and finally lined with brown satin so they glow from within. Five cocoons (and a moth) overlap the frame.

The scene was hand painted onto a cotton canvas and the trees and foreground were extensively machine embroidered. Beads were added to accentuate the setting sun. The small moths in flight are of appliquéd silk and satin, while some are just machine embroidered.

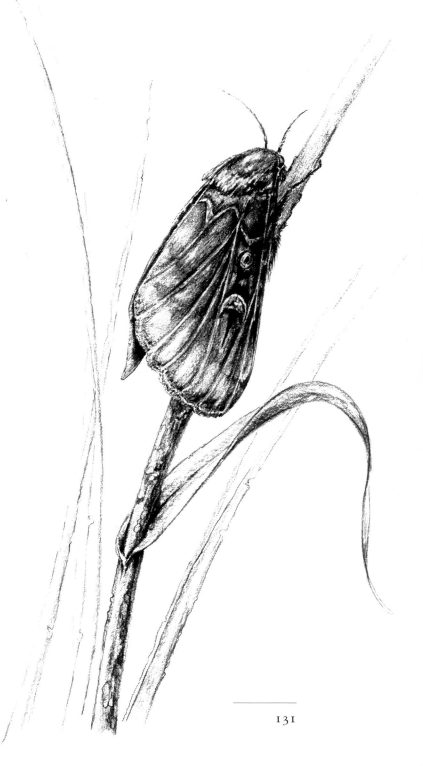

No. 52, *Fabric Fantasy*, details.

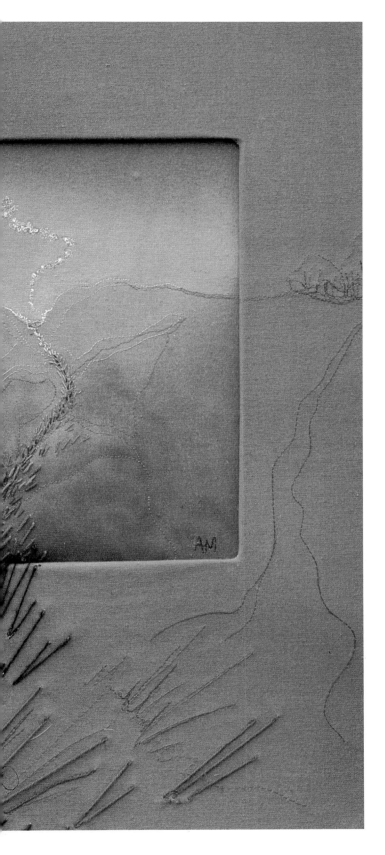

53
GRASSHOPPER FLIGHT
[1988]

High-relief wall sculpture
60 × 100 × 6 (relief) cm
Private collection

Walking through long grass at the height of the grasshopper season can be an intriguing experience, especially if one is trying to capture a choice specimen. Clouds of grasshoppers always seem to jump and fly just out of reach. This work was inspired by driving in a grassy paddock at dusk with one grasshopper (*Austracris guttulosa*) sitting on the inside of the windscreen.

Grasshopper Flight explores another way of using surface-plane layering techniques to achieve a window effect of 'inside looking out'. It was designed in two main parts. One canvas has a rectangular hole in it and was placed on top of the other. They were framed individually to achieve a neat finish and create the illusion of extra depth. The flow lines of the flying grasshoppers and grasses are in alignment and lead from one level of the canvas to the other in diminishing size. The grasses are hand sewn in embroidery wools and cottons, linking the two levels in a series of carefully measured straight stitches.

The paler tones of the inner panel give the appearance of bright light coming from behind the horizon, and this is accentuated by the shadows cast by the grasshopper wings on the hill. I used limited tones of blue, green and yellow throughout the work with sharp highlight contrasts introduced with white silk, silver-lustre textile paint and glass beads.

54
DANCE OF THE MAYFLIES
[1988]

High-relief wall sculpture with relief sections
extending beyond the frame
110 × 180 × 10 (relief) cm
Private collection

Dance of the Mayflies leans towards a mystical interpretation and mood-setting work rather than being a portrayal of mayflies that are absolutely correct in every anatomical detail or colour. For example, I improvised with the wing veining and insect colour schemes. Mayflies (Ephemeroptera) are so small, their wings so sheer and fine, that they appear to take on whatever colour surrounds them. I hope this work will arouse some awareness of these delightful and harmless insects.

Inspiration for the design was sparked by my visit to the commissioner's peaceful and tasteful apartment. There, in the centre of busy Melbourne, was an elegant and quiet place that lent itself magnificently to an environmentally orientated textile work.

My commissioner's longstanding home is in Gippsland so I chose to portray the local fauna in mayflies as a reminder of the region's abundant rivers and spectacular wetlands.

I wanted to complement and blend in with the existing and the proposed colour schemes. The apartment was not quite finished when the work was designed, but the brief allowed me plenty of scope. The colours in the textile were limited to blues, greens, pinks and mauves to suit the interior design and soft furnishings. The unbroken white wall on which the work is now displayed is 5 metres long and 2.6 metres high, and it is in a prominent position.

Dance of the Mayflies is the largest textile work I have made within one frame.

SCENE   The scene is set at dusk with the moon rising. The sky has a soft pink lustre. The heavily embroidered valley and tree line are deliberately contrasted with the relatively plain areas of the rest of the canvas. These simple areas add to the feeling of space, fragility and flight, and allow the mayflies to be the predominant feature.

Action lines have been added around the wings to increase the sense of movement and upward flight. They are in a variety of pale and dark threads to suit the moon's light and to merge the mayflies and their background environment smoothly.

I have included subtle small circular forms or bubbles on the backing to repeat the shape of the dominant moon, and also as a reminder that 99 per cent of a mayfly's life is restricted to being under water.

MAYFLIES Many different shades of glitter fabric, satin, silk and moiré taffeta were used under painted silk organza to give a sheen and subtly change the intensity of the colour tones on the wings. The three largest mayflies have about twelve different underlay fabrics between them.

All the layers of wing fabrics were attached to a fine layer of felt, with iron-on fabric fastened to the back, to avoid stretching the silk with intensive sewing. Each wing of each mayfly was made individually, and extensively machine embroidered for shadows and colour highlights, veins and patterns. The five main mayflies were each made in approximately fourteen separate parts — eyes, head, thorax, abdomen, wings, legs and 'tails'. That means there were about seventy parts for five mayflies.

The semi-relief angles and the texture of the wings were achieved by false-tension sewing and stress-steam moulding. False-tension sewing (with a tight bobbin tension and loose top thread tension) was used to embellish the wing fabric with squared scale-like, semi-relief puckers and indentations. The wings were then pulled and tugged under steam and pressure exerted with the point of the iron to mould their smoothly contoured wavy edges. Dacron wads were sewn under some high points to support their weight. One

wing required extra support to enable it to hang smoothly over the edge of the frame.

The heads, thoraxes and abdomens required a great deal of hand quilting to achieve the height of relief and texture that I desired and to avoid distorting or flattening them. These body parts are of satin, taffeta, silk and shaved-pile fur fabric. The long flowing 'tails' (cerci), and some antennae and forelegs, are made of hand-plied embroidery silk and cotton, graded according to colour and thickness requirements. These insect parts were attached to the canvas backing using a specially made foot for the machine with the centre bar cut and filed away so that they would lie flat and smooth without puckering.

The eyes are of covered fabric buttons, stitched on an angle to achieve a foreshortened effect.

Most of the small mayflies were outlined in stitches on two layers of painted silk organza; the last few, nearest the moon, are just machine stitches.

MOON This tiny but dominant feature of the whole design is made of five different layers of fabric. From back to front these are iron-on fabric, silver glitter fabric, yellow silk organza, cream organza and finally pale pink organza. The inner layers have been lightly quilted to give the textural effect of different levels while the pink silk organza overlay extends beyond the moon to soften its outline. The details on the ring around the moon were sewn on the machine, with tiny stitches of glitter thread added by hand later for highlights.

55
MAYFLY LIFE CYCLE
[1988]

High-relief wall sculpture
133 × 44 × 10 (relief) cm
Private collection

Mayflies (Ephemeroptera) began to intrigue me after I collected specimens at Lake Guthridge in Sale and then researched their life cycle for *Dance of the Mayflies*. This long, thin wall sculpture shows their aquatic life cycle from egg to nymph, and then subimago (or intermediate adult) to airborne adult.

The scientific name of the order, Ephemeroptera, stems from a Greek word meaning 'living a day'. As this suggests, these insects have a short adult life. They are unable to eat once they have emerged from the final nymphal moult. They die within hours of mating. Mayfly eggs are laid on water or submerged vegetation and become anchored by fine threads. They hatch as nymphs that feed under water and shed their skin up to twenty times. These nymphs can live up to three years. At the end of its aquatic life the nymph rises to the surface, its back splits open and a dull coloured, winged insect emerges. It cannot fly well at all. Shortly it splits again and the fully coloured adult with glittering translucent wings appears. This occurrence of a subimago is unique among insects.

Mayflies are known for their nuptial dances. Hundreds of thousands of them, mainly males, drift up and down with the air currents. When a female appears a male detaches himself from the flock and mates with her. Her body is literally an airborne egg sac that is crammed with eggs. The drama ends with the male falling to his death and the female just having enough time to release her fertilised eggs on the water. She dies, often floating on the water with outspread wings. Anglers frequently model their flies on species of mayfly as they are popular food for fish.

In Australia about one hundred and twenty-four mayfly species have been recorded and each has a distinctive habitat. These range from swamps to streams, lakes and rivers, and from lowlands to sub-alpine regions.

To my delight, this work was purchased by the owner of *Dance of the Mayflies*. They both hang in the same room and complement each other in colour and subject matter.

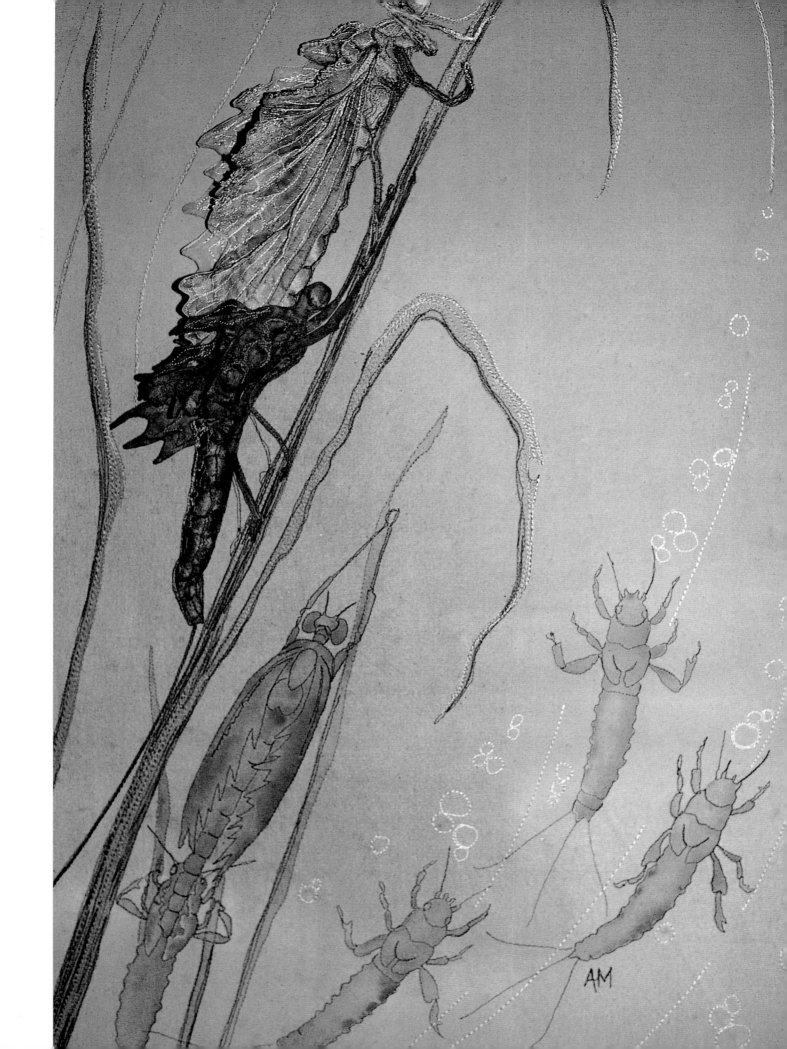

56
FROG DOWN UNDER
[1988]

High-relief wall sculpture
91 × 105 × 5 (relief) cm
Private collection

I have often wanted to repeat and enlarge a part of a work and, by so doing, create a different mood and emphasis in the new textile. I have done this in *Frog Down Under*. The initial frog design was drawn in 1980 and incorporated in the textile panel *Frogs*. It was used as a catalogue cover design in 1981 and a wine bottle label in 1988. Eight years after the initial design I wanted to re-express the elegance and agility of this delightful creature (*Litoria aurea*) in a more decorative and unashamedly feminine setting.

The frog's body, legs and toes were streamlined to make him more delicate and athletic. I particularly wanted to realistically reproduce the almost scaly, reptilian appearance of the frog's skin. After much trial and error with a variety of fabrics and threads, I perceived that sewing with an exceptionally tight bobbin tension and loose top thread tension – pushing this technique to the limit – caused a bubbling and dimpling that was ideal. This false-tension sewing was done on two layers of fine green silk organza, with a further layer of cream silk organza being added where the frog's body was to be paler in colour. Trapunto quilting was used to pad out areas such as the throat, abdomen and thighs to give them even higher relief.

The frog's supporting branch (*Eucalyptus sideroxylon*) was curved downwards for aesthetics and realism, to suggest his weight and precarious balance.

This work was a particular pleasure to create as I felt so challenged to improve on my earlier one. Side by side they are very different.

Frog Down Under was awarded the Textile Art Prize in the Wildlife Art Society of Australasia's 1988 annual exhibition in Melbourne. The judges' comments were:

The treatment of the frog with its legs meandering around the tree trunk was enchanting. The whole subject was beautifully composed and a mature work of art. The fact that this was textile art seemed to be forgotten when appraising same, however on closer examination the minute detailing of the whole was meticulously done and the sewing – superb. The colours were mutations of brown and green with a few other splashes of colour here and there for effect and the total effect was one of serenity. This was a world class piece of textile art. (*Wildlife Art Society of Australasia Newsletter*, Vol. 12, No. 4, November 1988)

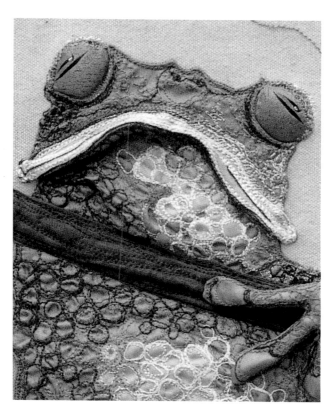

OPPOSITE AND ABOVE No. 56, *Frog Down Under*, details.

57
LEWIN HONEYEATER
NESTLINGS I
[1989]

High-relief wall sculpture
160 × 70 × 6 (relief) cm
Private collection

For large detailed wall works like this one, much of the time needed for its execution is spent on field work, collecting specimens, sketching and designing. Proportionately, this time is almost equal to the hours spent sewing. In *Lewin Honeyeater Nestlings I* I have tried to capture the beauty of our eucalypt-dominant bushlands, with eaten-out gum leaves, gum blossoms and two baby honeyeaters (*Meliphaga lewinii*) swinging in their delicately constructed nests.

At the time, some honeyeaters were nesting in a tree near my front door, so they conveniently became my subject for study. I aimed at portraying the subtle, muted, earthy colour tones of our bush – the browns, tans, olive greens and so on – and thus highlighting and focusing on the brilliant yellow interior of the bird's beak.

SCENE   The scene was sketched at Briagolong, then painted and stitched in many sequential stages in the studio. It is set before dawn in late summer. Over twenty different machine-thread colours were used to achieve the gradual changing of colours, highlights and shadows. The threads ranged from pure silk to cottons and some polyesters and glitter thread, all varying in thickness and tensions. A thin layer of dacron wadding was stitched to the back of the central trees to make them appear to be in low relief.

I have contrasted the heavily embroidered and detailed valley and tree line with relatively plain and bare areas in the rest of the background. It is all too easy to clutter a work of this size. The simple areas add to the feeling of space, fragility and balance and allow the eye to move freely around the design. Stitched outlines of leaf shapes were added to the canvas to increase the sense of movement and to subtly integrate low-relief areas with the plain canvas background.

BIRDS   The nestlings are depicted in two very characteristic positions: one is pulling its head in, looking fluffy, fat, well fed and a little sleepy, perhaps even annoyed by its sibling. The other, with a long stretched-out neck, is aggressive, noisy and demanding food. This action is causing the nest and branch to sway.

The parent bird is not in the picture, but I have tried to convey the feeling that it will arrive at any moment to feed the wide-open beak.

The birds' outlines were painted on cream silk organza, their shapes were supported with heavy felt, and the details were machine embroidered. Very little painted silk remains exposed after the intensive machine embroidery. All raw fabric edges were turned and stitched in to avoid future fraying. The semi-relief angles of the body shapes were achieved by hand quilting with dacron wadding as the inside padding. This was done by hand to avoid distorting the birds' shape.

Making the beaks, eyes, feathery breasts and specific facial expressions of the birds was very challenging. I wanted to make them aesthetically acceptable as baby birds without seeming too cute.

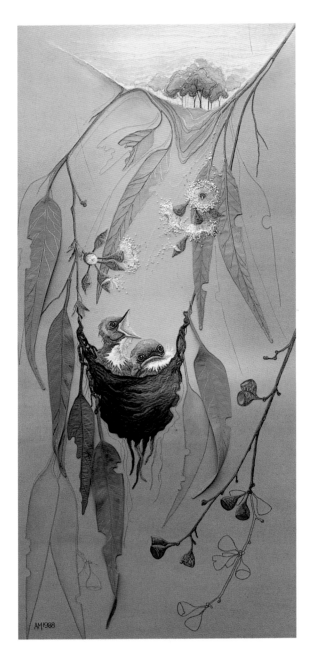

NEST The work shows the typical cup-shaped nest of the Lewin Honeyeater hanging among foliage. It was made by hand painting silk organza in shades of tan and brown, then placing the painted silk over an arrangement of many different coloured sewing threads and wools, which was backed with another layer of brown silk to support the loose threads. Free-sewing in straight stitch on the machine was used to simulate the woven twigs and cobwebs that bond a real nest together.

On the surface of the nest I have used the tailor-tacking foot to give a little added texture with a tangle of stitches. Small tubes of brown silk organza were turned inside out and woven around the nest's supporting branches to give a higher relief.

LEAVES The leaves are the typical elongated eucalypt shape with holes eaten out by caterpillars, colour blemishes and twists and curls.

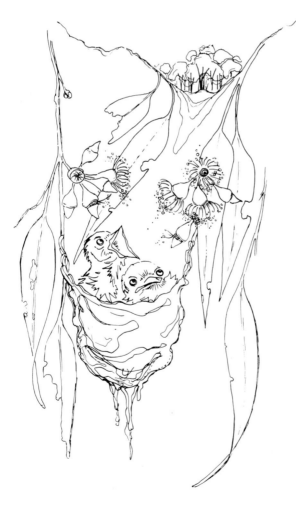

Mature Leaves Four different but toning shades of green gabardine were used in the six main leaves. The gabardine was also hand painted in small areas to give subtle colour gradings to some leaves. Several leaves were painted directly onto the canvas backing, while others are of separately painted canvas appliquéd onto the canvas surface.

All semi-relief leaves were reversed and embroidered with veins and blemishes before being attached to the work. Their narrow stems were difficult to turn inside out.

New Shoots A few new leaf shoots were incorporated as their green to orange colour tonings help balance the colours of the whole work.

The new shoots are made of two layers of silk organza, hand painted and machine embroidered for vein details. Some of them are so small that they could not be stitched on the machine as they would just disappear down into the bobbin case. They have been attached to the backing canvas only at the stems and by some veins, so as to be in semi-relief.

GUM BLOSSOMS All stages of gum blossom development are depicted in the work, ranging from developing buds, opening buds and full blooms to nuts. The blossoms were first hand painted on the canvas in cream and white textile paint, so that I could control their exact outline and placement. They were machine stitched in thick cream, white and yellow buttonhole threads. Then they were hand embroidered with thousands of French knots to create fluffiness.

A few French knots are 'floating in space' to give an added feeling of the branch swaying with the birds' actions. They also help lead the viewer's eye to the bird with the open beak.

STEMS AND BRANCHES The branches were designed to hang downwards, their flowing lines leading the eye to the focal area of the birds in the nest. They are quite stylised and used mainly to indicate the directional flow in the work's elongated shape. Each twig was hand painted then machine embroidered, with leaf stems attached at strategically designed points.

GUM NUTS The gum nuts were first painted directly onto the canvas and then machine embroidered with different intensities so that some appeared closer, others further away, some newer and others older. One small branch was only outlined in stitches to add to the overall balance and to ensure that the bottom of the work remained uncluttered.

58

BOOK ON LEWIN HONEYEATER NESTLINGS II

[1989]

32 × 26 cm
Husqvarna Sweden

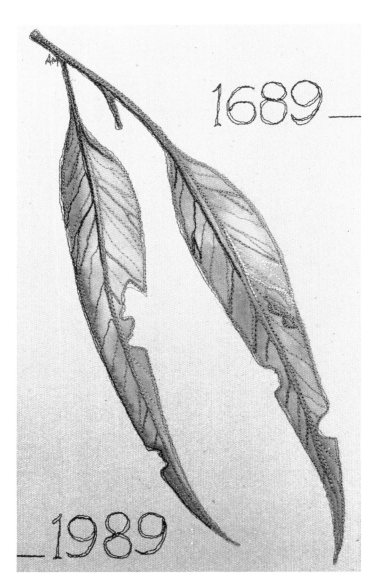

This textile book contains a step-by-step illustrated record of the processes involved in the creation of the small textile wall panel *Lewin Honeyeater Nestlings II* – a miniature version of *Lewin Honeyeater Nestlings I*. Both the book and the small panel were commissioned by the management and staff of Husqvarna Australia Pty Ltd for the 300th birthday of Husqvarna Sweden, and were designed to give the Swedish Sewing Academy a comprehensive understanding of all the procedures I go through. The book included inspirational ideas, design methods, layout plans, pattern drafting, fabric-painting techniques, machine and hand-embroidery techniques and nature notes.

Many of the pages were illustrated with fabric sewing samplers showing individual stages of making birds, gum blossoms, gum nuts and a nest. Other pages were illustrated with detailed photographs and sketches outlining complex procedures such as pattern drafting for relief work, silk painting, the sewing of large and awkward sections, and framing.

I have used Husqvarna sewing machines for nearly thirty years since my parents gave me a green Class 20 Husqvarna for my eighteenth birthday. For the past ten years Husqvarna Australia, and specifically Mr Ross Harper and Mrs Kath Caulfield, have been particularly helpful and supportive to me as a textile artist. Their encouragement, kindness, interest and friendship have been most gratifying. Consequently, when I was asked to make this book and textile wall work for Husqvarna's 300th birthday I was delighted and honoured.

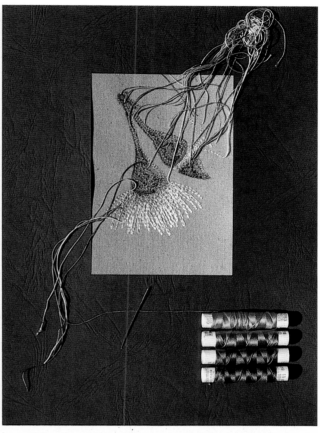

59
LEPIDOPTERA OLYMPIA AUSTRALIS
[1989]

Freestanding sculpture
55 × 49 × 12 (height) cm
Private collection

This sculpture was inspired by the magnificent Butterfly House at the Royal Melbourne Zoo and by the brief from Cato Design outlining their requirements for the 'Melbourne Olympic Bid Exhibition' for the 1996 Olympic Games.

To suit their display stands, the butterfly had to fit easily into a circle 60 centimetres in diameter, as their theme was 'The Rings of the Olympics'. Within the sculpture I have repeated the circular forms in both the insect's wing markings and surrounding cocoons. The display stand was angled backwards at 45 degrees, so this viewing angle had to be considered in the design.

Seven size-graded cocoons support the upward angle of the wings and so form a recess for the body of the butterfly, giving the appearance of imminent flight.

Construction techniques included dyeing merino, mohair and silk fibres, padding, quilting, pleating, trapunto, beading and machine embroidery. Metallic fabric and metallic machine threads were used extensively to give the brightly lit glittery effect.

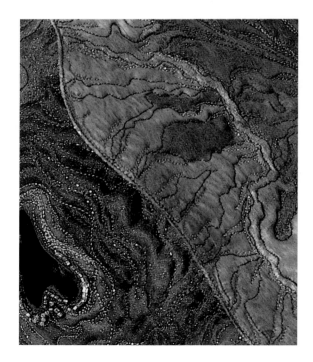

60
PHEROMONE FRENZY
[1989]

High-relief wall sculpture
155 × 120 × 10 (relief) cm
Private collection

*P*heromone Frenzy portrays a captivating personal experience. I was observing a group of pupal cases at soil level in long grass when one case split open before my eyes. With a great deal of leg kicking and delicate manoeuvring, the moth freed itself and prepared to pump up its wings. Within two or three seconds of emerging it was 'dive bombed' by another moth and fertilised. I have since learnt that many female moths send out a pheromone that can be detected by males at great distances.

The work depicts this moment before fertilisation – the urgency and fast flight of the male as he crashes into the picture and the female's scramble to freedom from the confines of her pupal case. The dozens of small distant moths are the ones that came too late. The sky is alive with them. My rendition of the moths is unrealistic in colour and species as I concentrated only on portraying the event and my astonishment at the speed of the encounter.

The male moth literally came 'out of the blue' so I chose blue for the predominant colouring of the work. Using textile paints, the cotton canvas was lightly washed in three separate stages to achieve a glowing back-lit appearance. Also, the underground hollow in the foreground was highlighted so that the pupal cases seem to be rising to light and life.

To establish flight action, speed and the airborne moth's purpose, I angled the beating wings to almost point at the emerging moth. Not all four wings can be seen equally. The wings that are only painted on the canvas and the stitched lines over and around them indicate where the wings were split-seconds before.

The moth's wings are of colour-graded and dyed merino and mohair wool underneath a fine layer of silk organza that was then embroidered on the machine. The eyes are satin-covered buttons, hand embroidered in fine silk for highlights. The antennae are of plied embroidery cottons and the thorax of the male moth is of blue dyed fur.

Two of the unhatched pupae are of dyed wools under silk organza and are padded with dacron. The others are combinations of painted, stitched or padded canvas.

Intensive hand stitching and machine-embroidery along the grass line contrasts with the finer line-stitching of the sky and pupal cases.

Because of its size, the work was made in two main parts then joined along the unravelled weft. It is designed to be viewed first from a distance so that the overall mood is established, and then more closely for the fine detail.

No. 60, *Pheromone Frenzy*, details.